pizza

NEW
HOLLAND

contents

introduction

Originating most likely in Naples as a simple flatbread, what we think of as 'pizza' is only one member of a family of traditional Italian bread-based foods that serve as a meal in one. As you'll discover, these flatbreads range from conventional Neapolitan versions to calzone and other variations – few Italian dishes are as familiar as pizza, or as irresistible.

The definition of a pizza is changing and this book features contemporary specialities with the emphasis on fresh and readily available ingredients. The result is an amazing variety of innovative pizzas that are as flavourful as they are enjoyable to make and eat.

THE MAKINGS OF A GREAT PIZZA

The best pizzas all have one thing in common: they are made from the best-quality ingredients.

Use a good grade of olive oil for pizza dough and cooked sauces. Save the finest grades (virgin or extra-virgin) for drizzling over pizza just before baking.

Use the best-quality cheese. Buy a block of aged Parmesan (not pre-grated (shredded)) and grate (shred) it just before using. Use fresh whole mozzarella cheese packed in its own whey, if available; otherwise use a premium brand of packaged whole mozzarella (not pre-sliced or pre-grated).

Use fresh herbs when possible; if you use dried herbs, purchase them in small quantities.

Use fresh garlic, prepared shortly before using. Garlic salt or powder does not provide the same flavour as fresh garlic.

ingredients

FLOUR

There are two main types of wheat grown today, hard and soft, each with a characteristic kernel composition and each with its own particular culinary use. The wheat kernel will vary in "hardness", which is the measure of protein content and consequently determines the flour's gluten content. Hard flour contains large protein chunks and relatively little starch. As a result this flour forms a strong gluten when mixed with water and is commonly used in bread making. In comparison soft flours contain a higher starch content and consequently develop a weaker gluten. Soft flours are more commonly used for pasta and cakes in which the texture is meant to be more tender and crumbly. Gluten works rather like chewing gum. It will change its shape under pressure and also tend to reassume its original shape when pressure is removed. Gluten stretches when worked and allows air to be incorporated and trapped, resulting in air bubbles in the dough. Bread making requires a hard flour in order for the carbon dioxide, released by the yeast, to be incorporated by the gluten, enabling the dough to rise. Pizza dough does not require the same level of rising action as a loaf of bread and many people claim that a softer flour is actually better. The following is a guide to the different flours available and their uses.

Semolina – a coarse grain produced from the hardest kind of wheat grown today. This is predominantly used for very stiff doughs, particularly dried pastas. It is too hard for bread or pasta making but can be added to pizza doughs for texture and crunch.

Hard flour – grade 1 contains the highest gluten level and is generally used for bread making or pizzas.

Soft flour – grade 00 (*doppio zero*) is the finest grade and contains less gluten. It is useful for pasta making and baking. Soft flour can be used for pizza making but make sure the packet states that it is "panifiable", meaning that it is suitable for bread making.

YEAST

Yeasts are a group of single-celled funghi and about 160 different species are known. It is one species in particular, *Saccharomyces cerevisiae* or "brewer's sugar fungus", that is good for brewing and baking. Yeast gives off a characteristic flavour and smell; it leavens bread (meaning it causes it to ferment and rise) and converts the grain carbohydrates into alcohol and carbon dioxide. When we buy fresh yeast it is live but inactive. With a little warmth and the addition of some water it is activated and releases the gas — carbon dioxide — that will raise the dough. The activity ceases only when the dough is placed in the oven and the yeast is killed by extreme heat.

Fresh yeast – this should be putty-like in colour and texture; it should look firm and moist and feel cool to the touch. If it is dry, dark and crumbly it may be stale or not live. Fresh yeast can be bought for a pittance from many supermarkets that have a bakery on site or from your local bakery. Keep fresh yeast in an airtight container in the refrigerator for up to 3 days. Alternatively, divide the yeast into 15 g or 30 g (½ oz or 1 oz) portions and freeze it for up to 3 months. Always defrost the yeast thoroughly at room temperature or in the refrigerator before use.

To use: using a spoon, crumble the fresh yeast into a small glass bowl and add about a quarter of the required amount of water as specified in the recipe. Use the back of the spoon to cream the yeast until it dissolves in the water and forms a smooth blended paste. Stir in the remaining water. The yeast mixture is now ready to be added to the flour.

Dried granular yeast – usually bought in glass jars from the supermarket. Dried yeast can be reconstituted with a little lukewarm water and will give exactly the same result as fresh yeast. It must be stored in an airtight container. Always keep an eye on the date stamp. If it doesn't produce a frothy head when reconstituted with water it is not fresh.

To use: sprinkle dried granular yeast into a small glass bowl containing the quantity of lukewarm water specified in the recipe. Leave to dissolve for 5–10 minutes. Once the yeast has dissolved, stir the mixture with a wooden spoon. The yeast mixture is now ready to be added to the flour. Continue as instructed in the recipe.

Dried easy-blend yeast – the easiest of yeasts to use as it is just added to the flour, with the water added separately. Again, the end product will be just as superior as if it were made using fresh or granular yeast. Always check the date stamp to ensure freshness.

To use: sprinkle dried easy-blend yeast directly onto the flour. The yeast will activate once the liquid has been added. Continue as instructed in the recipe. Easy-blend yeast cannot be used for the "sponge" method.

NOTES
- 15 g (½ oz) fresh yeast = 2 tsp dried granular yeast = 2 tsp dried powdered yeast

- In the recipes we have used dried granular yeast and the method has been written to reflect this. If you want to use other types of yeast when making the recipes, refer back to these pages.

PIZZA BASES

There is great satisfaction to be had in making your own pizza bases. Not only is the kneading process a great way to relieve tension in your body but the end result will also taste better than any bought alternative! It is important, when making bread, to understand your ingredients and what they do in order to achieve the best result possible. Environmental factors such as temperature and humidity will all play a part, as will the age of the flour you use, the hardness of the water you incorporate and the freshness of the yeast. One single bread-making experience will never be the same as the next. If the dough feels a little dry then add more liquid; if it is too wet then add a little more flour. With practice you will become familiar with how it should look and feel and will develop an instinct for adding a little more of one ingredient and a little less of another. As always, these recipes are guidelines to which you can adhere as much or as little as you like. If you are pressed for time, there are alternatives to making your own base which can make your pizza-making experience quick and easy and with a delicious end result.

PIZZA DOUGH MAKING

Mixing – this involves the mixing together of flour, water and yeast – as simple as that. Once mixed the gluten proteins begin to unfold and form water-protein complexes. Secondly, the yeast begins to feed on the sugars in the flour and starts the process of fermentation and the production of carbon dioxide. In some recipes we use a "sponge" method, which involves mixing up to half of the flour in with the yeast and water mixture. This can give a slightly more aerated end product due to the longer time of fermentation.

Kneading – this improves the aeration of the dough and furthers the development of the gluten. It is best done by hand if you prefer a product with larger air bubbles, though some bread machines and food mixers do have dough hooks, which will create bread with a very fine, cake-like texture. Your technique for kneading will determine the final texture of your pizza base. Your dough is well kneaded when it takes on a silky, satiny appearance. Rich, buttery or sweet doughs generally require longer kneading than others.

Rising (fermentation) – the stage when the dough is set aside and covered with a clean tea (kitchen) towel in a warm place. The gluten development is still happening but the main activity is the multiplication of yeast cells, which causes the dough to rise and expand. The yeast is producing more carbon dioxide which, in turn, expands the air pockets resulting in the final bread texture. The dough should approximately double in size and then it is ready. At this stage it is important to knead (punch back) the dough to release the pressure, shape it and leave it for another short rising. Then it is ready to be rolled out and topped.

Baking – when the dough is initially put in the oven it will experience a sudden expansion as the heat will cause a rapid production of carbon dioxide. When the interior of the dough reaches about 60°C (140°F) the yeast cells will die and the rising will cease. The dough will then undergo a phase of browning that will give the dough its crispy texture. Perfectly cooked dough should sound hollow when tapped.

FREEZING DOUGH

Your dough can be frozen as dough balls after the rising (fermentation) stage. Just knock the dough back, reshape into a ball and place in a freezer bag. Remove the dough from the freezer about 6–8 hours before you need it. Leave it to defrost at room temperature. When you are ready, turn the plastic bag inside out and, using a floured hand, pull the dough from the bag. Knead the dough on a lightly floured surface for 5 minutes. Shape into a ball and leave for 20 minutes before rolling it out.

PIZZA BASE ALTERNATIVES

Pitta bread – use pitta breads to make mini or individual pizzas, which are great for the kids. Let them top their own and experiment with the ingredients.

Tortillas – these make a thin and crispy base. These can also be cooked in a frying pan and even topped with a second tortilla to make a quesadilla. Great served as a quick finger-food snack chopped into wedges.

Naan bread – choose an Indian-inspired topping, such as spinach and paneer cheese, and finish it off with an authentic naan bread base. This is a breadier alternative to tortillas.

Puff pastry – it's hard to say whether making a pizza with puff pastry is cheating or not. Most of us would call this a tart but it's basically the same concept and a quick and easy alternative if you buy ready-rolled sheets.

Bought bases – bought pizza bases come in many shapes and forms and are available from all good supermarkets. Try frozen, vacuum-packed or ready-rolled bases from the chiller cabinet. Some supermarkets or delicatessens may sell frozen balls of pizza dough, which just require defrosting, and shaping. Alternatively, your local Italian restaurant may sell you frozen balls of dough.

OLIVE OIL

We've used extra virgin olive oil in our recipes. Olive oils vary considerably in taste and strength. Choose one with a flavour you like. In some cases we use infused olive oils, such as chilli or basil oil.

Infused oils – you can buy these or make your own. To infuse oils, firstly wash and dry your chosen herb or spice and lightly bruise it (put pressure on it) to release the flavour. Place the herbs or spices in a clean, sterilized jar or bottle and cover with warmed oil. Seal tightly and leave in a cool, dark place to infuse for about 2 weeks. Leave the herbs and spices in if you want a stronger flavour or a decorative look, otherwise strain. Use the oils within 2 months of initial bottling. Some suggested flavourings are basil, chilli, rosemary, thyme, tarragon, cardamom, star anise or cloves.

TOMATOES

There are more than 5,000 varieties of tomato in the world today varying from yellow cherry tomatoes and green plum tomatoes to red beef tomatoes. Tomatoes transform white pizza bread into a rich and flavourful meal. Italian cooking without tomatoes would truly be unthinkable. Tomatoes can be bought in many varieties: fresh, tinned, puréed, sun-dried and semi-dried are all readily available today. Tomatoes are made up of about 94 per cent water and must always be well drained, whether fresh or tinned, in order to avoid a soggy pizza.

Canned tomatoes – these are scalded, peeled and slightly salted before being canned. Canned tomatoes are a very popular choice for pizza makers today and are of equal quality to the fresh variety. In many cases it is the superior, unblemished tomatoes that are sent away for canning when the not so perfect tomatoes are left behind for fresh sale.

Tomato purée – many professional pizza makers steer clear of tomato purée, arguing that it tends to dull the other flavours, making all pizzas taste the same. We're not sure if this is truly the case and it is certainly a useful ingredient if you want to assemble a pizza in a hurry.

PREPARING TOMATOES

When you select fresh tomatoes for topping a pizza or making pizza sauce, choose varieties that have a high proportion of flesh to seeds and juice; these are often labelled as plum, pear or paste tomatoes. Select tomatoes that are fragrant and fully ripe and keep them out of the refrigerator if you want to maintain peak flavour.

1. Use a paring knife to core the tomatoes. Turn the tomatoes over and slit the skin in an X-shaped cut.
2. Put the tomatoes in a pan containing enough boiling water to cover them and boil for 15 seconds. Remove them with a slotted spoon and put them in a bowl of cold water. Leave for a few seconds.
3. Remove them from the cold water and use a paring knife to pull off the skins. Halve the tomatoes horizontally with a chopping knife. Hold each half over a bowl, cut side down, and squeeze to remove the seeds. Chop the tomatoes into small pieces.

CHEESES

Mozzarella – *mozzarella di bufala* is the original mozzarella and is delicious served as is. It is sweet in flavour and soft in texture but does not melt as well as cow's mozzarella. Cow's milk mozzarella is the one to use for cooking. It has a very mild, creamy and faintly sour flavour and melts beautifully, making it ideal for pizzas. Mozzarella can also be made with goat's milk, which is a little sharper in taste and is not such a popular choice.

Mozzarella is produced as a semi-soft, fresh cheese or a firm block of cheese made with low-or non-fat milk. The fresh cheese is the ultimate choice for home-made pizzas but it is important to make sure you drain and dry it well to remove as much excess moisture as possible. Fresh mozzarella balls are usually packaged in water or, brine or whey, to preserve freshness. Fresh mozzarella is mild in flavour, soft and very pliable. The longer that mozzarella ages the softer and sourer it becomes. In all our recipes we have used fresh mozzarella unless otherwise specified.

Mozzarella can also be found in other forms:

- **Block mozzarella** – block mozzarella is lower in moisture than fresh mozzarella and is often the preferred choice for many commercial pizza makers. In America as many as 90 per cent of all commercial pizza makers will use block mozzarella. It is lower in fat and consequently not as flavoursome as fresh mozzarella.
- **Bocconcini** – small mozzarella balls usually about 2.5 cm (1 in) in diameter.
- **Mozzarella affumicata** – *affumicato* means 'smoked' in Italian. This cheese is lightly smoked over wood chips and is darker in colour than standard mozzarella.
- **Mozzarella scamorza** – this mozzarella has been heavily smoked, usually over pecan shells, and is much darker in colour and denser in texture.
- **Mozzarella pearls** – tiny balls of mozzarella, which are about 1.5 cm (⅝ in) in diameter. They are available from some supermarkets but if you can't find them then a large mozzarella ball cut into cubes is exactly the same.

Mozzarella can be wrapped in plastic food wrap (cling film) and frozen for up to 3 months. Frozen mozzarella does decrease in flavour and may become moister in texture. Before serving or cooking allow the cheese to defrost in the refrigerator before removing and warming to room temperature. Fresh mozzarella usually keeps for up to 2 weeks when chilled.

Parmesan

When buying Parmesan always look for the words *Parmigiano reggiano* for authenticity and quality. Never buy pre-grated (shredded) or shaved Parmesan in tubs. It is important to keep Parmesan from drying out so always buy a freshly cut piece and grate (shred) it only when needed. Parmesan cheese is rich and round in flavour and has the ability to melt with heat and become inseparable from the ingredients to which it is added. To store Parmesan for longer than 2–3 weeks divide it into pieces, each with a piece of rind still attached, and wrap tightly in greaseproof paper (baking paper), then in heavy duty aluminium foil. Store on the bottom shelf of the refrigerator.

Pecorino

The Italian word for sheep is *pecora*, hence all cheese made from sheep's milk is called pecorino. There are dozens of pecorinos available: some are soft and fresh while others are crumbly and sharp, more like a Parmesan.

Fontina

Fontina is a semi-hard cheese with a creamy texture and subtle nutty flavour. It is a very useful cheese for cooking as it has good melting properties, making it a popular choice in fondues and pizzas. Fontina is made from unpasteurized cow's milk from the grazing cows of the Val d'Aosta alpine region of Italy.

Ricotta

The word *ricotta* literally means 'recooked' in Italian. It is made from the whey of other cheeses that is cooked again to make a milky white, soft, granular and mild tasting cheese. Ricotta does not melt.

Gruyère

Gruyère is a firm cheese with a nutty flavour. It works best when finely grated (shredded).

Asiago

A semi-firm to hard Italian cheese with a nutty, sharp flavour that is mainly used for grating (shredding). Asiago was traditionally made with sheep's milk, but it is now more commonly made with cow's milk.

Havarti
Havarti is a mild, semi-soft Danish cheese with small irregular holes.

Monterey Jack
Monterey Jack is a type of Cheddar-style cheese first made in California using pasteurized cow's milk. It is commonly sold by itself, or mixed with Colby cheese to make a marbled cheese known as Colby-Jack (or Co-Jack).

Cheddar
Choose a mature Cheddar for the best flavour and always grate (shred) for use on pizza to get a more even melt.

Provolone
This is a southern Italian cheese that is pale yellow in colour, with a smooth texture. Milder, fresh provolone can be eaten on its own, although once aged it is generally used in cooking.

Gorgonzola
Gorgonzola is a mild and creamy blue-veined cheese. Choose dolcelatte if you prefer a creamier, milder soft blue cheese.

Taleggio
Taleggio is a semi-soft cheese made from whole cow's milk. Its flavour can range from mild to pungent, depending on its age. When young, the colour of taleggio is pale yellow. As it ages it darkens to deep yellow and becomes rather runny. Taleggio is sold in blocks and is covered either with a wax coating or a thin mould.

Mascarpone
Mascarpone is a soft, unripened cheese that belongs to the cream cheese family. It comes from northern Italy and is a thick, rich, sweet and velvety, ivory-coloured cheese produced from cow's milk that has the texture of sour cream. It is sold in plastic tubs and can be found in most delicatessens and good supermarkets.

CURED MEATS

Prosciutto

Prosciutto is the pig's hind thigh or ham that has been salted and air-dried. The salt draws off the meat's excess water, thus curing and preserving it. A true prosciutto is never smoked. When served it should always be thinly sliced and used as soon as possible. If you are not consuming it immediately then each slice or each single layer of slices must be covered with greaseproof (baking) paper or plastic wrap (cling film) then wrapped in aluminium foil. Prosciutto is delicious eaten as it is or cooked on pizzas. It can be quite salty so do not add extra salt unless needed.

Pancetta

Pancetta is from the pig's belly and is the Italian equivalent of bacon. Pancetta can be bought sliced or cubed and is more tender and considerably less salty than prosciutto. It can also be eaten raw or cooked. Pancetta is rarely ever smoked except in a few areas of northern Italy.

Salami

Salami is the generic term for cured and fermented meat (usually pork or beef) that is typically flavoured with spices such as black pepper, fennel, chilli or paprika. The meat mixture is ground and stuffed into casings then hung to dry, either in hot or cool air, until the sausages have reduced in weight by at least half. Some salamis or cured sausages will additionally be smoked. Examples of common salamis and cured sausages are Napoli, Milano, Genoa, chorizo and pepperoni.

Mortadella

Mortadella can be used sliced or diced on pizzas. It is made from the lean shoulder and neck meat from carefully selected pigs and is then studded with the creamy fat from other parts of the pig. Mortadella is often flavoured with a blend of spices and condiments that varies from producer to producer.

Bresaola

Bresaola is very thinly sliced, cured and air-dried lean beef. It is gently spiced to develop its rich and aromatic flavour.

PREPARING GARLIC

Choose fresh whole garlic heads that look plump and feel firm. Avoid heads that are withered or have bruised or darkened cloves. Store in a cool, dry, dark place with good air circulation. Try to leave the heads whole until you are ready to use them; cloves that have been separated from the head dry out rapidly and should be used as soon as possible.

1. Put a garlic clove on a board. Hold the flat side of a large knife just above it. Lightly pound the knife, hitting the garlic and loosening its skin. Pull the skin off, cutting if necessary.
2. Return the garlic to the board and position the knife above it as in step 1. Hit the blade vigorously with the side of your fist to crush the garlic.
3. To chop the garlic, cut it several times in one direction. Then slice it against the direction of the first cut. Continue until very finely chopped.

ROASTING RED CAPSICUMS

Throughout Italy, Spain and southern France, cooks roast sweet red capsicums (bell peppers) and serve them as a salad or add them to a variety of dishes. A few strips of roasted red capsicums add vibrant colour and flavour to pizza. Although bottled roasted red capsicums are widely available, preparing them yourself is simple and far more economical.

1. Hold the capsicums over an open gas flame or charcoal fire, (use a pronged instrument to hold them, or place them under a grill (broiler). Turn often until blackened on all sides. Transfer the capsicums to a plastic bag; close and set aside until cool (15–20 minutes).
2. Peel the capsicums, then halve them and remove the stem and seeds. Arrange the halves flat and use the dull side of a small knife to scrape away any black bits of skin and stray seeds. Slice into ¼ in (6 mm) strips.

Equipment & methods

COOKING METHODS

The wood-fired oven

This is an essential factor in the creation of the true Neapolitan pizza. The design of the traditional wood-fired pizza oven is more than 2,000 years old. These ovens are dome-shaped, made from brick or clay, and the roof is heated by direct contact with the flames from the burning wood below. The dome shape then causes the heat to be reflected back down to the base of the oven.

In a well-used oven (such as those in many pizzerias in Naples) the fire will never go out completely – even when there are no pizzas in the oven. The flames will die right down and just embers will be left burning so the oven can be bought back up to temperature at a much faster rate. A pizza oven will reach about 400°C (750°F), at which temperature a pizza will cook in about 1½ minutes. If you are lucky enough to have a wood-fired oven the woods of choice are cherry or olive wood, as they don't smoke as much as other woods. Make sure you also invest in a long pizza paddle to get your pizzas in and out of the deep oven.

Wood-fired ovens are becoming more and more popular as an outside alternative to a barbecue. They are used to cook a wide variety of foods, not just pizzas. Whole large roasts and loaves of bread can be successfully cooked in them as well as semi-dried tomatoes, zucchinis and other vegetables.

The conventional oven

For a while electric ovens were beginning to replace the traditional wood-fired oven in many pizzerias around the world. It seems today that the wood-fired oven may be making a comeback in most pizzerias but for many of us an electric or gas-fired oven is still the practical main oven of choice. With such an oven we have a lot more control over temperature and this makes it more suited to most domestic homes. Although the flavour and smell may not be quite as authentic as that of a wood-fired oven, the pizza that you will produce can still be of top quality. It may be worth investing in a pizza stone if you are planning on doing some serious pizza making at home. All our recipes are tested in fan-assisted ovens, which produce a crisper, golden crust.

The pizza stone

A pizza stone will transform your electric or gas oven into the modern equivalent of the clay and brick ovens used by traditional pizza bakers. Cooking pizzas on such a stone gives them a crispness that cannot otherwise be achieved from an oven. Most pizza stones have been fired at temperatures in excess of 1,100°C (2,000°F). This enables them to give a very dry heat that is also evenly distributed, eliminating any hot spots and giving a consistent browning to the pizza. Pizza stones are suitable for use in both gas or electric ovens. Try serving your pizza directly on the stone and it will stay hot right through until the last slice. It is important always to heat your pizza stone first so it can absorb the heat of the oven. You will need a pizza paddle or use our parchment paper technique to transfer your topped pizza quickly on to the stone without losing too much heat – alternatively, you will need to work very quickly to assemble your topping. Sprinkle a little flour on the pizza stone first to stop it sticking. Be very careful when handling the stone as it gets very hot and will remain hot for a long time.

In our recipes we have said to use a baking sheet as not everyone will have a pizza stone, but obviously if you have one use it instead.

The barbecue

Cooking pizza on the barbecue is a great way to impress your guests. It requires no special skills, just the flick of the switch or some burning coals. It's a good idea to keep a supply of frozen pizza dough balls in the freezer for those spontaneous summer evenings. Just defrost the dough, roll it out and within minutes you can have a crisp, slightly charred crust with your chosen topping. Some topping ingredients, such as bunches of cherry tomatoes or grilled eggplants (aubergines), are best cooked separately. Let the cheese melt on the base and throw the extra topping on – hey presto!

OTHER EQUIPMENT

Pizza paddle

If you own a wood-fired oven or a pizza stone then a pizza paddle is definitely worth investing in. Always lightly flour it before setting the dough on it so that it can easily be transferred to the oven or on to the pizza stone.

Thermometer

If you are lucky enough to own a wood-fired oven then a good thermometer is essential in order to judge the inside temperature of the oven. Choose one that reaches a temperature of at least 400°C (750°F).

Pizza plates

If you don't have a pizza stone on which to serve your pizza then you will need to buy a few flat, round plates for serving. Alternatively large chopping boards will suffice.

Pizza cutter

A pizza cutter definitely speeds up the cutting process.

Baking parchment

Baking parchment can be very useful to help transfer your topped pizza on to your baking sheet or pizza stone. Make sure the paper is lightly floured and just roll out your pizza dough on it as you would on any other surface. Slide the paper and dough onto the pizza stone or baking sheet and leave the paper there during cooking.

Ladle

Useful for transferring sauce from the bowl to the pizza base. Then use the base of the ladle to distribute the sauce around the base, ensuring you leave a 1–2 cm (½–¾ in) border. Most of our pizzas call for 125 ml (4fl oz) of sauce so try buying a ladle that fits this volume exactly.

RECIPE INFORMATION

• All pizza recipes make one pizza unless otherwise specified and generally serve 1–2 people.

• For all our recipes we have given our preferred choice of base and sauce.

• All our recipes have been tested in a fan-assisted oven. If you are using a conventional oven then increase our recommended cooking temperature of 220°C/425°F/Gas mark 7 to 240°C/475°F/Gas mark 9. All ovens vary in performance so always check that your pizza is cooked to the desired crispness before serving.

• Keep your pizza toppings simple and the result will always be better.

• Unless otherwise stated, pizzas should always be served straight from the oven while the base is still crispy.

• Always use floured work surfaces and hands when working with pizza bases.

• In all our recipes we have used fresh mozzarella unless otherwise specified.

Basic doughs & sauces

Making pizza dough from scratch gives you complete control over the flavour and texture of the foundation of every good pizza – the crust. From a sturdy hand-kneaded Neapolitan dough to one that practically makes itself in an automatic breadmaker, here we present a collection of basic doughs and crusts. From this book you can build an impressive pizza repertoire.

Basic pizza dough

MAKES 1 PIZZA CRUST

1½ teaspoons dry yeast
pinch sugar
10½ fl oz (325 ml/1⅓ cups) warm water
  (about 105°F/41°C)
4 fl oz (120 ml/½ cup) olive oil

1 lb (450 g/4 cups) plain (all-purpose) flour,
  sifted
1¼ teaspoons salt
olive oil, for bowl, as needed

1. In a small bowl dissolve the yeast and sugar in the warm water and let stand for 5 minutes. Stir in the olive oil. In a large bowl combine the flour and salt. Add the yeast mixture and stir until the dough just barely holds together.
2. Turn the dough out onto a lightly floured surface and knead until smooth and silky, adding a little more flour if the dough seems sticky. Put the dough in an oiled bowl and turn to coat the surface with oil. Cover the bowl with cling wrap (cling film) and leave to rise in a warm place until doubled in bulk (about 1 hour).
3. After the dough has risen, punch it down, using your fist in a straight-down motion.
4. To shape into pizza crust, on lightly floured surface, roll the dough out to the desired size. Place on a baker's peel or oiled pizza pan dusted with cornmeal. Any excess dough can be wrapped in plastic kitchen wrap (cling film) and kept in the refrigerator.

NOTE: A simple, straightforward dough enriched with oil, this one is ready to use in a little more than an hour. For a firm, elastic dough that yields a crisp, finely textured crust, replace up to half the flour with semolina, a high-protein flour ground from hard durum wheat.

Wholemeal pizza dough

MAKES 1 PIZZA CRUST

8 oz (225 g/2 cups) plain (all-purpose) flour
2 oz (50 g/½ cup) wholemeal (wholewheat)
*   flour*
7 g (¼ oz) dry yeast
½ teaspoon salt

8 fl oz (250 ml) 1 cup very warm water (about
*   120°F/50°C)*
1 teaspoon honey
2 teaspoons olive oil

1. In a large bowl of a heavy-duty electric mixer, combine 6½ oz (175 g/ 1⅔ cups) of the plain flour, all the wholemeal flour, yeast and salt. Stir to blend the dry ingredients thoroughly.
2. In a small bowl combine the water, honey and oil, stir to blend well. Add the water mixture to the flour mixture. Mix to blend, then beat at medium speed until smooth and elastic (about 5 minutes). Stir in half of the rest of the plain flour to make a soft dough.
3. Turn the dough out onto a well-floured board or pastry cloth. Knead until smooth and elastic (5–10 minutes), adding just enough flour (up to 2 oz (55 g/½ cup) to prevent the dough from being sticky.
4. Place the dough in an oiled bowl and turn to coat evenly. Cover with cling wrap (cling film) and leave to rise in a warm place until doubled in bulk (30–40 minutes).
5. Punch down the dough, cover with an inverted bowl, and let rest for 10 minutes.
6. On a lightly floured surface, roll out the dough to the desired size. Place on a baker's peel or oiled pizza pan dusted with cornmeal. Any excess dough can be wrapped in plastic kitchen wrap (cling film) and kept in the refrigerator.

NOTE: Wholemeal flour produces a dense, chewy crust with a hearty, satisfying flavour. Doughs containing wholemeal flour tend to rise more slowly than those made with plain flour, but using fast-rising active dry yeast reduces the rising time by about half. This recipe calls for a heavy-duty electric mixer, but you can mix the dough by hand.

Neapolitan pizza dough

MAKES 1 PIZZA CRUST

¼ oz (7 g) dry yeast
½ pint (300 ml/1¼ cups) warm water (about 105°F/41°C)
10 oz (275 g/2½ cups) plain (all-purpose) flour
½ teaspoon salt

1. In a medium bowl dissolve the yeast in the water. Add half of the flour and mix well to make a sponge or soft batter-like dough. Cover with cling wrap (cling film) and leave to rise for about 45 minutes.
2. In a large bowl, combine the remaining flour and the salt. Add the risen dough and mix well. Turn out onto a lightly floured surface and knead until smooth and silky (about 5 minutes), adding flour as necessary. Put the dough in an oiled bowl and turn to coat evenly. Cover and leave to rise for 2 hours.
3. Punch down the dough using your fist in a straight-down motion.
4. To shape into pizza crust, on lightly floured surface, roll out the dough to the desired size. Place on a baker's peel or oiled pizza pan dusted with cornmeal. Any excess dough can be wrapped in plastic kitchen wrap and kept in the refrigerator.

NOTE: This classic Neapolitan pizza dough yields a dry crisp crust that can support a moist topping, such as fresh clams. The recipe contains no oil other than which is used for oiling the bowl and the dough prior to rising. Allowing the dough to rise twice produces a pleasing, yeasty flavour.

Food processor pizza dough

MAKES 1 PIZZA CRUST

10 oz (275 g/2½ cups) plain (all-purpose)
flour
¼ oz (7 g) fast-rising active dry yeast
¼ teaspoon salt
8 fl oz (250 ml/1 cup) very warm water
(about 122°F/50°C)

1 teaspoon honey
2 teaspoons olive oil

1. In the bowl of a food processor fitted with a steel blade, mix the flour, yeast and salt. Combine the water, honey and olive oil in a measuring cup. With the processor running, pour the water mixture through the feed tube in a steady stream, adjusting the amount poured so the flour can absorb it. Turn the processor off when the dough gathers into clumps and before it forms a smooth ball. Do not over process – it should feel sticky. If it is too soft, add more flour, 1 tablespoon at a time, until the dough has a firm consistency.
2. Knead by processing for an additional 45 seconds or knead by hand until the dough is smooth and silky. Shape into a ball.
3. Place the dough in an oiled bowl and turn to coat evenly. Cover with cling wrap (cling film) and leave to rise in a warm place until doubled in bulk (30–40 minutes).
4. Punch down the dough, cover with the inverted bowl, let rest for 10 minutes.
5. To shape into pizza crust, on lightly floured surface, roll the dough out to the desired size. Place on the baker's peel or oiled pizza pan dusted with cornmeal. Any excess dough can be wrapped in plastic kitchen wrap and kept in the refrigerator.

NOTE: A food processor fitted with a steel blade can mix pizza dough in seconds. If your food processor is powerful enough to handle heavy yeast doughs without damaging the motor, you can also use it to knead the dough. If necessary, mix the ingredients in the food processor and complete the kneading by hand.

Breadmaker pizza dough

MAKES 1 PIZZA CRUST

¾ cup water
2 fl oz (75 ml/⅓ cup) olive oil
1¼ cups semolina flour
1¼ cups plain (all-purpose)
½ teaspoon salt
1½ teaspoon dry yeast

1. Place all the ingredients in the pan of a breadmaker in the order given (follow the manufacturer's instructions). Put the pan in the breadmaker and select the setting for mixing dough.
2. When the dough cycle is complete, remove the dough from the breadmaker pan then shape as desired. Alternatively, place the dough in a plastic bag and refrigerate for up to two days before shaping.

Making pizza dough in an automatic breadmaker takes almost no effort. You simply place the ingredients in the bread pan that comes with the machine, and the dough is automatically mixed, kneaded and raised at a controlled temperature. When the timer on the machine indicates that the cycle is complete (after about an hour or so), you remove the dough, shape it into a crust, and top and bake it as you would any pizza. For specific instructions on the order of ingredients and setting the machine for mixing and raising pizza dough, consult the manufacturer's manual for your specific bread machine. The semolina flour produces a chewy crust with a crisp exterior.

Deep-dish pizza dough

MAKES 1 DEEP-DISH PIZZA CRUST

12 oz (350 g/3 cups) plain (all-purpose) flour
¼ oz (7 g) fast-rising active dry yeast
¾ teaspoon salt
½ pint (300 ml/1¼ cups) very warm water (about 120°F/50°C)
2 teaspoons honey
1 tablespoon olive oil

1. In a large bowl combine 10 oz (275 g/2½ cups) of the flour with the yeast and salt. Stir to blend the dry ingredients thoroughly. In a small bowl combine the water, honey and oil, and stir to blend well.
2. Add the water mixture to the flour mixture. Mix to blend, then beat by hand or with an electric mixer set at medium speed until smooth and elastic (about 5 minutes). Stir in the rest of the flour to make a soft dough.
3. Turn the dough out onto a floured board or pastry cloth. Knead until smooth and satiny (8–10 minutes), adding more flour if the dough is sticky.
4. Place the dough in an oiled bowl and turn to coat evenly. Cover with cling wrap (cling film) and leave to rise in a warm place until doubled in bulk (30–40 minutes).
5. Punch down the dough, cover with inverted bowl, and let rest for 10 minutes.
6. To shape into pizza crust, on a lightly floured surface, roll out the dough to the desired size. Place on a baker's peel or oiled pizza pan dusted with cornmeal. Any excess dough can be wrapped in plastic kitchen wrap and kept in the refrigerator.

NOTE: Traditional deep-dish pizzas are baked in a special high-sided pan that resembles an oversized cake pan (tin). This recipe makes enough dough to line a pan about 15 in (37 cm) in diameter and 2 in (5 cm) deep. If you prefer a crust that is crisp on the outside, with a chewy interior, replace up to half of the plain flour with semolina.

Cheese pizza dough

MAKES 1 PIZZA CRUST

1½ teaspoons dry yeast
1½ tablespoons olive oil
½ teaspoon sugar
10 oz (275 g/2½ cups) plain (all-purpose) flour
2 oz (55 g) mature Cheddar cheese, grated (shredded)
1 teaspoon salt

1. Place the yeast, oil, sugar and ¼ pint (150 ml/⅔ cup) warm water in a large bowl and mix to dissolve. Set aside in a warm, draught-free place for 5 minutes or until foamy.
2. Put the flour, cheese and salt in a food processor and pulse once or twice to mix. With the machine running, slowly pour in the oil and yeast mixture and process to form a rough dough. Turn the dough out onto a lightly floured surface and knead for 5 minutes or until soft and shiny. Add more flour, if necessary.
3. Lightly oil a large bowl, then roll the dough around in it to cover the surface with oil. Cover tightly with cling wrap (cling film) and place in a warm, draught-free place for 1½–2 hours or until doubled in volume. Punch down and remove the dough from the bowl. Knead briefly before using as desired.

Herb pizza dough

MAKES 1 PIZZA CRUST

1½ teaspoons dry yeast
½ teaspoon sugar
1½ tablespoons olive oil
1o oz (275 g/2½ cups) plain (all-purpose) flour
1 teaspoon dried mixed herbs
1 teaspoon salt

1. Put the yeast, sugar, oil and ¼ pint (150 ml/⅔ cup) warm water in a large bowl and mix to dissolve. Set aside in a warm, draught-free place for 5 minutes or until foamy.
2. Put the flour, herbs and salt in a food processor and pulse once or twice to sift. With the machine running, slowly pour in the oil and yeast mixture and process to form a rough dough. Turn the dough onto a lightly floured surface and knead for 5 minutes or until soft and shiny. Add more flour, if necessary.
3. Lightly oil a large bowl, then roll the dough around in it to coat the surface. Cover the bowl tightly with cling wrap (cling film) and place in a warm, draught-free place for 1½–2 hours or until the dough has doubled in volume. Knock down and remove dough from bowl. Knead briefly before using as desired.

Tomato pizza dough

MAKES 1 PIZZA CRUST

1½ teaspoons dry yeast
1½ tablespoons olive oil
½ teaspoon sugar
¼ pint (150 ml/⅔ cup) tomato juice, warmed
10 oz (275 g/2½ cups) plain (all-purpose) flour
1 teaspoon salt

1. Place the yeast, sugar and tomato juice in a large bowl and mix to dissolve. Set aside in a warm, draught-free place for 5 minutes or until foamy.
2. Put the flour and salt in a food processor and pulse once or twice to mix. With the machine running, slowly pour in the oil and yeast mixture and process to form a rough dough. Turn the dough onto a lightly floured surface and knead for 5 minutes or until soft and shiny. Add more flour, if necessary.
3. Lightly oil a large bowl, then roll the dough around in it to coat the surface with oil. Cover tightly with cling wrap (cling film) and place in a warm, draught-free place for 1½–2 hours or until dough has doubled in volume. Knock down and remove the dough from the bowl. Knead briefly before using as desired.

Basic tomato sauce

MAKES 4 FL OZ (120 ML/½ CUP)

3 tablespoons chopped fresh basil
½ teaspoon dried oregano
1½ tablespoons white wine
¼ medium onion, grated (shredded)
1 clove garlic, chopped
1 teaspoon olive oil
2 tomatoes peeled, deseeded and chopped
1½ teaspoons tomato paste (purée)

1. In a small bowl, steep (infuse) the basil and oregano in white wine for 10 minutes.
2. In a frying pan over medium-high heat, sauté the onion and garlic in olive oil for 5 minutes, stirring frequently. Add the tomatoes and tomato paste, then the herbs and wine. Cover, reduce the heat and simmer for 15 minutes.
3. Remove the sauce from the heat and purée in a blender or food processor.

NOTE: The secret to the flavour of this quick, low-fat sauce is steeping the basil and oregano in wine before cooking. This simple step draws out the flavour of the herbs, creating a sauce that tastes as if it has been cooking for hours. This recipe calls for fresh tomatoes, but you may also use canned varieties.

Spicy pizza sauce

MAKES 2 CUPS

1 tablespoon olive oil
½ onion, finely chopped
½ red capsicum (bell pepper), chopped
1 clove garlic, chopped
1 teaspoon chilli flakes
1 small red chilli, chopped
14 oz (400 g) can chopped tomatoes
2 tablespoons tomato paste (purée)
1 teaspoon dried oregano

1. In a saucepan, heat the oil over medium heat, add the onion, capsicum and garlic. Cook, stirring often until the ingredients are soft.
2. Mix in the chilli flakes, chilli, tomatoes, tomato paste and oregano. Bring to the boil and cover for about 15 minutes.
3. Uncover, increase the heat and stir until the sauce thickens and reduces, about 10 minutes.

Pesto pizza sauce

MAKES 1 CUP

2 cups fresh basil leaves, loosely packed
2 fl oz (50 ml/¼ cup) olive oil
2 tablespoons pine nuts, toasted
2 cloves garlic, chopped
½ teaspoon salt
1 oz (30 g) Parmesan, freshly grated (shredded)
1 oz (30 g) romano cheese, freshly grated (shredded)

1. Put the basil, olive oil, pine nuts, garlic and salt in a blender or food processor. Blend or process until smooth.
2. Transfer to a bowl and stir in the Parmesan and romano cheeses.

NOTE: The pungent, licorice-like aroma and flavour of basil makes a mouth-watering tomato-less sauce. In the summer, farmers' markets and roadside stands in many areas offer several different varieties of basil that can be used to make an assortment of pestos, each with its own distinctive flavour and colour. You could also substitute fresh spinach for the basil. Pesto also marries nicely with pasta, rice or even fresh Italian or French bread.

Garlic-oregano pizza sauce

MAKES 1 CUP

6 cloves garlic, finely chopped
¼ cup fresh oregano, chopped
4 fl oz (120 ml/½ cup) dry white wine
4 fl oz (120 ml/½ cup) olive oil
salt and freshly ground black pepper
freshly grated (shredded) Parmesan cheese

1. In a small saucepan over low heat, cook the garlic, wine and half the olive oil until the garlic is very soft, about 30 minutes. The mixture will have the consistency of a rough paste.
2. Spread the paste on the pizza dough. Drizzle with the remaining olive oil and sprinkle with oregano. Season with salt, pepper and Parmesan.

Rouille sauce

MAKES ½ CUP

1 tablespoon dry white wine
pinch of ground saffron
2 teaspoons olive oil, plus 2 fl oz (50 ml/¼ cup)
⅛–¼ teaspoon crushed hot chilli flakes
1 egg yolk
1 teaspoon fresh lemon juice
½ clove garlic, chopped
pinch of salt
¼ cup fresh basil, chopped

1. Mix the wine and saffron and steep (infuse) in a small bowl for 10 minutes. Heat 2 teaspoons of the oil in a small frying pan. Add the chilli flakes and cook for 10 seconds. Remove the pan from the heat and add the wine and saffron mixture (stand back – it will sizzle). Leave to cool.
2. In a small mixing bowl, whisk the egg yolk with the lemon juice, garlic and salt. Gradually begin adding the rest of the olive oil, drop by drop, whisking continuously. As the sauce begins to thicken, add the oil a little faster. When all the oil is added, stir in the chilli mixture and basil.

Anchovy & herb sauce

MAKES ¾ CUP

1 clove garlic
4 oz (115 g/½ cup) mayonnaise
1 teaspoon mustard
1 tablespoon drained capers
3 anchovy fillets
¼ cup basil leaves
3 stalks parsley

1. Crush and peel the garlic. Place in a food processor or blender with the mayonnaise, mustard, capers, anchovies, basil and parsley. Process or blend until smooth. Serve on the side.

Cheddar-horseradish sauce

MAKES 4 CUPS

1 oz (30 g) butter
2 tablespoons plain (all-purpose) flour
1 teaspoon mustard powder
16 fl oz (475 ml/2 cups) milk
2 eggs, beaten
3 oz (85 g) mature Cheddar cheese, grated (shredded)
3 tablespoons prepared horseradish
½ teaspoon dried dill
1 teaspoon chopped canned pimento

1. Melt the butter in a saucepan over medium heat. Add the flour and mustard and stir briskly until a paste forms. Add the milk in a thin stream, whisking all the while, until the mixture is smooth and thickened.
2. Pour half of the mixture into a small bowl and whisk to cool. Whisking constantly, slowly pour the beaten eggs into the white sauce, then slowly pour the egg mixture into the saucepan, whisking constantly until thickened, about 10–15 minutes.
3. When thickened, smooth and glossy, add the remaining ingredients, stir to blend and add salt to taste. Add more horseradish if desired. Serve warm.

Fiery sauce

MAKES 4 CUPS

2 lb (900 g) ripe tomatoes, finely chopped
10 fresh hot chillies, chopped
4 cloves garlic, chopped
3 onions, finely chopped
2 stalks celery, finely chopped
1 tablespoon olive oil
2 fl oz (50 ml/¼ cup) distilled vinegar
2 tablespoons sugar
¼ cup coriander (cilantro) leaves, very finely chopped
½ teaspoon freshly ground black pepper

1. In a blender, purée a handful of the chopped tomatoes with as many chillies as can be accommodated. Continue until all chillies have been puréed. Pour into a large pot. Add the rest of the tomatoes and remaining ingredients.
2. Cook over high heat for 10 minutes, stirring frequently to avoid scorching. Reduce the heat to moderate and cook, stirring occasionally, until the salsa is thickened, about 45 minutes. Season to taste with salt, more sugar or vinegar and crushed dried chillies. Cook for 10 minutes more.
3. Let cool, spoon into storage containers and refrigerate or freeze.

Fruit & vegetable

Sun-dried tomatoes have a sweet intensity that's almost candy-like. Just a few, cut in strips, will enrich and enliven a topping with fresh tomatoes. Add some sweet, height-of-summer red capsicums and you have a delicious bright red topping for a warm-weather pizza.

Pizza caponata

MAKES 1

1 medium eggplant (aubergine), unpeeled
4 fl oz (120 ml/½ cup) olive oil
2 onions, thinly sliced
1 celery, stalk
4 oz (115 g/½ cup) tomato purée
6 cloves garlic, chopped
2 tablespoons pine nuts, toasted

2 tablespoons sugar
4 fl oz (120 ml/½ cup) red wine vinegar
salt and freshly ground black pepper
½ cup flat leaf parsley, chopped
2 oz (55 g/½ cup) chopped black olives
1 quantity basic pizza dough (see page 34)
1½ oz (45 g) Parmesan, grated (shredded)

1. Cut the eggplant into ¾ in (2 cm) cubes. In a large frying pan over moderately high heat, heat 4 tablespoons of the oil. Add the eggplant and sauté until lightly browned and softened. Transfer the eggplant to absorbent paper to drain.
2. In the same frying pan over moderate heat, sauté the onions in 2 tablespoons oil until soft but not browned. Add the celery, tomato purée and garlic and simmer for 10 minutes.
3. Add the toasted pine nuts, sugar, vinegar, salt, pepper and parsley. Add the eggplant and simmer for 15 minutes. Remove from the heat and stir in the olives.
4. Preheat the oven to 450°F/230°C/Gas mark 8.
5. Shape the pizza dough and top with eggplant mixture. Drizzle with a little more olive oil and sprinkle with Parmesan. Bake until well-browned, about 20 minutes. Serve hot.

Pizza rossa

MAKES 1

1 tablespoon olive oil
4 cloves garlic, chopped (see page 24)
2 tomatoes peeled, deseeded and chopped (see page 17)
¼ cup fresh basil, chopped
1 quantity Neapolitan pizza dough (see page 38)
2 red capsicums (bell peppers), roasted
1½ tablespoons sun-dried tomatoes, sliced
1 tablespoon oil from sun-dried tomatoes
1 oz (30 g) Parmesan, coarsely grated (shredded)

1. Preheat oven to 475°F/240°C/Gas mark 9.
2. In a large frying pan heat the olive oil over moderately low heat. Add the garlic and sauté gently until fragrant but not browned, about 3 minutes. Add the fresh tomatoes and basil, stir to mix and remove from the heat.
3. Shape the pizza dough and brush lightly with extra olive oil. Spoon the fresh tomato mixture over the dough and top with roasted red capsicums. Garnish with sun-dried tomatoes. Drizzle with oil from the sun-dried tomatoes and dust with Parmesan.
4. Bake until browned and bubbly, about 18 minutes.

Pizza al pesto

MAKES 1

1 quantity Neapolitan pizza dough (see page 38)
3 oz (85 g) mozzarella cheese, grated (shredded)
1 quantity pesto pizza sauce (see page 56)
2 tablespoons pine nuts

1. Preheat the oven to 475°F/240°C/Gas mark 9.
2. Shape the pizza dough and arrange the cheese over the dough. Spoon pesto over the cheese. Garnish with pine nuts and bake until browned and bubbly (about 18 minutes). Serve hot.

Pizza alla funghi

MAKES 1

1 quantity basic pizza dough (see page 34)
6 marinated artichokes or artichoke hearts, quartered
4 oz (115 g) mushrooms, thinly sliced
2 oz (55 g) Parmesan, grated (shredded)
1 oz (30 g) mozzarella cheese, grated (shredded)
2 spring onions (scallions), finely chopped
freshly ground black pepper
1 tablespoon olive oil

1. Preheat the oven to 450°F/230°C/Gas mark 8.
2. Shape the pizza dough and arrange the artichokes on top. Add the mushrooms, Parmesan, mozzarella, spring onions and pepper. Drizzle with olive oil. Bake until well-browned and puffy, about 20–25 minutes.

Chicago-style vegetarian pizza

MAKES 1

1 head garlic
2 tablespoons olive oil
1 quantity deep-dish pizza dough (see page 44)
1 bunch spinach, washed and drained
1 green capsicum (bell pepper), sliced
1 quantity basic tomato sauce (see page 53)
4 oz (115 g) mozzarella cheese, grated (shredded)
1½ oz (45 g) Cheddar cheese, grated (shredded)

1. Preheat the oven to 350°F/180°C/Gas mark 4.
2. Place the garlic bulb in a small baking dish and pour 2 tablespoons of oil over it. Bake until the garlic is tender, 50–60 minutes. Cool slightly and set aside.
3. Increase the oven temperature to 450°F/230°C/Gas mark 8. Grease a 15 in (37 cm) deep-dish pizza pan and line with dough. Bake for 5 minutes and remove from the oven.
4. Meanwhile chop the spinach coarsely and cook in a frying pan over medium-high heat until wilted. Remove the spinach and reserve.
5. Squeeze the garlic from the papery shell over the pizza dough. Arrange the spinach, capsicum, sauce and cheeses over the dough. Bake until the cheeses are melted and the crust is lightly browned, 20 minutes.

Original tomato pizza

MAKES 2

2 quantities basic pizza dough (page 34)
olive oil
5 ripe tomatoes, sliced
4 cloves garlic, sliced (see page 24)
½ cup fresh oregano leaves
freshly ground black pepper

1. Preheat the oven to 400°F/200°C/Gas mark 6. Divide the dough into two portions and shape each into a 12 in (30 cm) round. Place the rounds on lightly greased baking sheets and brush with oil.
2. Arrange half the tomato slices, garlic and oregano on top of each pizza base and season to taste with black pepper. Bake for 15–20 minutes or until base is crisp and golden.

Pancetta & pear pizza

MAKES 4

1 quantity basic pizza dough (page 34)
5 oz (150 g) pancetta or prosciutto, thinly sliced
1 firm pear, cored, peeled and sliced
4 oz (115 g) creamy blue cheese such as Gorgonzola, crumbled
2 oz (55 g) walnuts, chopped
4 oz (115 g) rocket (arugula), roughly chopped
2 tablespoons balsamic or red wine vinegar
freshly ground black pepper

1. Preheat oven to 400°F/200°C/Gas mark 6. Divide the dough into four portions and shape each to form a 6 in (15 cm) round. Place the rounds on lightly greased baking trays (sheets) and cover with pancetta or bacon.
2. Arrange the pear slices attractively on top of the pancetta or prosciutto, then sprinkle with cheese and walnuts. Bake for 15–20 minutes or until the base is crisp and golden.
3. Just prior to serving, toss the rocket with vinegar and pile on top of the pizzas. Season to taste with black pepper and serve immediately.

Prosciutto & fig pizza

MAKES 4

1 quantity basic pizza dough (see page 34)
2 teaspoons olive oil
4 oz (115 g) prosciutto
4 fresh or dried figs, sliced
2 oz (55 g) pine nuts
2 sprigs fresh rosemary, leaves removed and chopped
freshly ground black pepper

1. Preheat the oven to 375°F/190°C/Gas mark 5. Divide the dough into four portions and shape each to form a 6 in (15 cm) round. Place the rounds on lightly greased baking trays (sheets).
2. Brush the dough with oil and top with prosciutto and fig slices. Sprinkle with pine nuts, rosemary and black pepper to taste, and bake for 15 minutes, or until bases are crisp and golden.

Crispy wholemeal pizza

MAKES 2

4 oz (115 g) wholemeal (whole-wheat) flour, sifted

3 oz (85 g) plain (all-purpose) flour, sifted

1 teaspoon sugar

¼ oz (7 g) active dry yeast

4 tablespoons olive or vegetable oil

TOPPING

2 tablespoons olive or vegetable oil

2 onions, chopped

2 cloves garlic, crushed

15 oz (400 g) can tomatoes, undrained and mashed

¼ cup fresh basil, chopped

2 small red chillies, deseeded and chopped

1 green capsicum (bell pepper), diced

12 oz (350 g) can unsweetened pineapple pieces, drained

6 stuffed olives, sliced

8 oz (225 g) mozzarella cheese, grated (shredded)

1. To make the base, place the flours, sugar and yeast in a large mixing bowl. Make a well in the centre, add 4 fl oz (120 ml/½ cup) warm water and the oil and mix to a soft dough. Turn the dough onto a lightly floured surface and knead for 10 minutes. Place the dough in a lightly oiled bowl, cover with cling wrap (cling film) and set aside in a warm place to rise for 30 minutes or until dough has doubled in size. Punch dough the down and knead on a lightly floured surface until smooth. Divide the dough in half. Roll out each half to fit a lightly greased 8 in (20 cm) pizza trays.
2. Preheat the oven to 400°F/200°C/Gas mark 6.
3. For topping, heat the oil in a large frying pan and cook the onions and garlic for 4–5 minutes, or until the onions are soft. Add the tomatoes, basil and chillies and simmer, uncovered, for 15–20 minutes or until the mixture reduces and thickens. Spread half the tomato sauce over each pizza base, then top each with half the capsicum, pineapple and olives, and sprinkle with mozzarella cheese. Bake for 20 minutes, or until the base is crispy and golden.

Grilled capsicum & pesto pizza

MAKES 2

2 red capsicums (bell peppers), deseeded and cut into quarters
2 green capsicums (bell peppers), deseeded and cut into eights
2 yellow capsicums (bell peppers), deseeded and cut into eights
4 baby eggplants (aubergines), halved lengthwise
1 quantity basic pizza dough (see page 34)
2 tablespoons olive oil
6 oz (175 g/¾ cup) pesto
3 oz (85 g) grated (shredded) Parmesan cheese

1. Preheat the oven to 425°F/220°C/Gas mark 7.
2. Brush the capsicums and eggplant with oil and bake in a lightly greased baking tray for 3–4 minutes each side or until soft and golden. Set aside.
3. Divide the dough into two portions and roll each into 8 in (20 cm) rounds. Place each on a pizza tray and cook for 3–5 minutes or until brown and crisp. Turn over, spread with pesto, top with roasted capsicums and eggplant and sprinkle with Parmesan.
4. Bake for 4–6 minutes longer or until pizza crust is crisp, golden and cooked through.

Pumpkin & feta pizza

MAKES 4

1 tablespoon olive oil
8 large slices pumpkin, peeled and seeds removed
1 onion, sliced
1 quantity basic pizza dough (see page 34)
10 oz (300 g) feta cheese, crumbled
4 sprigs fresh thyme, leaves removed and stalks discarded
freshly ground black pepper

1. Preheat the oven to 425°F/220°C/Gas mark 7.
2. Heat the oil in a frying pan over high heat until hot, add the pumpkin and onion and cook for 5 minutes each side or until soft and golden. Set aside.
3. Divide the dough into four portions and roll into rounds ⅛ in (3 mm) thick. Place the dough rounds on a pizza tray and cook for 3–5 minutes or until brown and crisp. Turn over, top with pumpkin, onion, feta cheese, thyme and black pepper, to taste, and cook for 4–6 minutes longer or until pizza crust is crisp, golden and cooked through.

Mushroom pizza

MAKES 1

1 quantity basic pizza dough (see page 34)
1 tablespoon olive oil
10 oz (300 g) salsa
1 onion, sliced
3 oz (85 g) mushrooms, sliced
3 oz (85 g) maturre Cheddar cheese, grated (shredded)
salt and freshly ground black pepper
4 sprigs oregano, leaves removed and chopped

1. Preheat the oven to 425°F/220°C/Gas mark 7.
2. Shape the pizza dough into a 12 in (30 cm) round. Place on a lightly greased baking tray (sheet) and brush with oil.
3. Spread liberally with salsa, then add the onion and mushrooms. Drizzle with more olive oil and cover liberally with the cheese, salt and pepper and oregano.
4. Cook for 20–25 minutes, until crispy.

Potato & red onion pizza

MAKES 8

16 fl oz (475 ml/2 cups) warm water
1 sachet dried yeast
1 teaspoon caster (superfine) sugar
2 lb 3 oz/1 kg strong bread flour (2 lb/900 g
    for dough, 3½ oz/100 g extra)
1 tablespoon extra virgin olive oil
1 teaspoon sea salt

TOPPING
2½ tablespoons chilli oil
4 potatoes, thinly sliced
2 small red onions, thinly sliced
3 sprigs rosemary, leaves removed
    and chopped
3½ oz (100 g) rocket (arugula) leaves
1½ oz (45 g) Parmesan, grated (shredded)

1. To make the pizza dough, combine the warm water with the yeast and sugar in a bowl and add 14 oz (400 g) of the flour. Stir until the mixture is a sloppy paste. Gradually add the rest of the flour, then the oil and salt, and work together with your hands until the mixture forms a ball. Knead the dough with your hands for 10 minutes until very elastic and smooth.
2. Put the dough in a lightly greased bowl, cover with a damp cloth and leave in a warm place for 2 hours, or until doubled in size.
3. Preheat the oven to 475°F/240°C/Gas mark 9. Dust a baking tray (sheet) with flour.
4. Cut the dough into 8 equal pieces. Dust the worktop with flour, roll out each piece of dough into rounds 3 in (7.5 cm) in diameter.
5. Place each on the baking tray and brush with the chilli oil, then top with potato, onion and rosemary. Repeat with the remaining dough and toppings, then bake for 5–10 minutes or until brown. Top with rocket and Parmesan, drizzle with a little oil and serve.

Pumpkin pizza

MAKES 2

1 quantity basic pizza dough (see page 34)
½ cup basic tomato sauce (see page 52)
3½ oz (100 g) pumpkin, diced and roasted
2 oz (55 g) feta cheese, crumbled
2 sprigs mint, chopped

1. Preheat the oven to 350°F/180°C/Gas mark 4.
2. Divide the pizza dough in two and roll out each piece to make two small pizza bases.
3. Spread each with tomato sauce. Top with the roasted pumpkin, feta and mint. Bake for 15–20 minutes until golden brown.

Pizza San Domenico

MAKES 4

12 oz (350 g) plain (all-purpose)
1 sachet dried yeast
4 tablespoons olive oil
1 teaspoon salt
1 teaspoon sugar

TOPPING
7 oz (200 g) tomatoes, skinned (see page 17)
3 tablespoons olive oil
6 cloves garlic, thinly sliced (see page 24)
7 oz (200 g) mozzarella cheese, sliced
freshly ground black pepper
2 oz (55 g) Parmesan, grated (shredded)
fresh marjoram sprigs

1. To make the dough, sift the flour into a bowl and mix in the dried yeast. Add the olive oil, salt, sugar and 4 fl oz (120 ml/½ cup) lukewarm water. Mix to a dough, then knead for about 5 minutes, until smooth. Cover and set the dough aside in a warm place until risen and doubled in size.
2. Knead the dough again, then divide into four equal pieces. Roll out each piece to form an 8 in (20 cm) round pizza base. Place on a greased baking sheet. Fold up the edge of each pizza base to form a raised rim and brush the dough with olive oil.
3. For the topping, slice the tomatoes and drizzle with olive oil, then arrange the slices over the pizza bases.
4. Top with the garlic, then the slices of mozzarella cheese and season with pepper. Leave the pizzas in a warm place to rise again.
5. Preheat the oven to 375°F/190°/Gas mark 5. Sprinkle over the Parmesan cheese, then bake for 15 minutes, until risen and golden brown. Serve garnished with fresh marjoram sprigs.

Tomato & zucchini pizza

MAKES 12

1 tablespoon fresh yeast
10 oz (300 g) wholemeal (whole-wheat) flour
2 tablespoons olive oil
½ teaspoon salt
1 bunch fresh parsley, finely chopped
2 cloves garlic, thinly sliced
10 oz (300 g) small zucchini (courgettes), sliced
10 oz (300 g) small tomatoes, sliced
10 oz (300 g) mozzarella cheese, diced
freshly ground black pepper
¼ cup fresh basil, finely chopped

1. Dissolve the yeast in 2–3 tablespoons of lukewarm water. Mix the flour in a bowl with the yeast mixture, ¼ pint (150 ml/⅔ cup) lukewarm water, 1 tablespoon olive oil and the salt. Knead the herbs and garlic into the dough. Cover the dough and set aside in a warm place for about 1 hour, until risen and doubled in size.
2. When the dough has risen, divide into 12 equal portions and roll or form into 12 small thin pizza bases. Place on two baking trays.
3. Preheat the oven to 400°F/200°C/Gas mark 6.
4. Cover six pizzas with zucchini, and six with tomatoes, then top each pizza with cheese and season with salt and pepper.
5. Bake for 25–30 minutes. When cooked, sprinkle with the remaining oil and garnish with chopped basil. Serve hot.

Cheese & onion pizza

MAKES 1

1 lb (450 g) wholemeal (whole-wheat) flour
1 sachet dried yeast
1 teaspoon ground coriander
1 teaspoon sea salt
1 teaspoon ground caraway seeds
2 eggs
¼ pint (150 ml/⅔ cup) lukewarm milk
2½ oz (65 g) butter, melted then cooled

TOPPING
1 oz (30 g) butter
14 oz (400 g) Roma tomatoes, sliced
7 oz (200 g) onions, finely chopped
4 fresh chillies, deseeded and sliced
7 oz (200 g) Emmental cheese, grated
  (shredded)
4 tablespoons Parmesan
2–3 teaspoons caraway seeds

1. For the dough, sift the flour into a mixing bowl and mix in the dried yeast, ground coriander, salt, ground caraway seeds, eggs, milk and butter. Knead to form a smooth dough, then cover and set aside in a warm place until risen and doubled in size. Knead the dough again, then roll out onto a buttered baking tray. Set aside.
2. For the topping, melt the butter in a frying pan, add the onions and cook until softened. Set aside to cool.
3. Preheat the oven to 400°F/200°C/Gas mark 6.
4. When cool, arrange the onions, tomatoes, chillies and cheese on the pizza base, then sprinkle with caraway seeds.
5. Bake for about 20–25 minutes. Serve hot.

Vegetable pizza

MAKES 2

½ butternut squash, peeled, cut into ½ in
  (12 mm) cubes
1 red capsicum (bell pepper), cut into ½ in
  (12 mm) pieces
1 yellow capsicum (bell pepper), cut into ½ in
  (12 mm) pieces
1 red onion, sliced
3 small zucchini (courgettes), sliced

2 tablespoons olive oil
2 teaspoons balsamic vinegar
salt and freshly ground black pepper
1 quantity basic pizza dough (see page 34)
½ cup tomato passata
4 oz (115 g) feta, crumbled
⅓ cup basil leaves

1. Preheat the oven to 400°F/200°C/Gas mark 6.
2. In a large bowl, toss the pumpkin, capsicums, onion and zucchini with oil,
   then season.
3. Fit the vegetables, but not the zucchini, on a large baking tray (sheet) in a
   single layer. Bake for 10 minutes, then add the zucchini to the tray and bake
   for 10 minutes, or until the pumpkin is tender and capsicums are a little
   charred at the edges. Place all the vegetables in a large bowl and toss with
   balsamic, then set aside.
4. Divide the dough in half and roll each half out to make an 8 in (20 cm) pizza
   base. Place on clean baking trays. Spread the bases with passata and top
   with roasted vegetables, reserving any balsamic.
5. Top with feta and bake for 15–20 minutes or until the feta is golden. Toss
   the basil in the reserved balsamic and scatter over pizzas to serve.

Mixed capsicum pizza

MAKES 1

1 quantity basic pizza dough (see page 34)
1 quantity basic tomato sauce (see page 52)
1 red capsicum (bell pepper), deseeded and cut into thin slices
1 green capsicum (bell pepper), deseeded and cut into thin slices
1 yellow capsicum (bell pepper), deseeded and cut into thin slices
7 oz (200 g) mozzarella cheese, sliced
salt and freshly ground black pepper
1 teaspoon dried marjoram
1 teaspoon olive oil

1. Preheat the oven to 425°F/220°C/Gas mark 7. Roll out the dough on a lightly floured work surface. Place on a lightly greased pizza tray.
2. Spread the tomato sauce over the dough and arrange the mixed capsicum slices evenly on top.
3. Place slices of cheese over the capsicum. Season with salt and pepper and scatter over the marjoram.
4. Drizzle over the olive oil and bake for 10–15 minutes until golden brown and bubbling.

Artichoke pizza

MAKES 1

8 oz (225 g) wholemeal (whole-wheat)
   self-raising (self-rising) flour
3 oz (85 g) butter
½ teaspoon salt
olive oil
1 tablespoon tomato purée
7 oz (200 g) can artichoke hearts, drained
   and halved

2 medium tomatoes, skinned and sliced (see
   page 17)
1 teaspoon dried oregano
4 oz (115 g) Cheddar cheese, finely sliced
12 black olives, pitted and halved

1. Preheat the oven to 375°F/190°/Gas mark 5. Mix the flour, butter and salt together in a large bowl and add enough warm water to make a pliable dough.
2. Roll out the dough into a 10 in (25 cm) round and place on a greased baking tray (sheet).
3. Brush with olive oil and spread with tomato purée. Arrange the artichokes and tomatoes on top and scatter with oregano.
4. Arrange the cheese over the tomatoes and place the olives on top.
5. Bake for about 35 minutes.

Meat & poultry

These pizzas will be adored by anyone looking for fresh ideas and interesting food. Pizzas are often associated with rich creamy sauces, masses of cheese and lots of olive oil. The recipes in this chapter keep these ingredients to a minimum while still retaining the traditional tastes of these ever popular foods.

Pizza parma

MAKES 1

1 quantity basic pizza dough (see page 34)
4 oz (115 g) prosciutto, thinly sliced
2 red capsicums (bell peppers), roasted and sliced (see page 24)
1½ oz (45 g) mozzarella cheese, grated (shredded)
1½ oz (45 g) Parmesan, grated (shredded)
¼ cup flat leaf parsley, finely chopped
olive oil

1. Preheat the oven to 450°F/230°C/Gas mark 8.
2. Shape the pizza dough, roll out into a round and fit on a lightly greased baking tray (sheet).
3. Arrange slices of prosciutto on the surface of the dough. Add the capsicums and cover with mozzarella, Parmesan and parsley. Drizzle olive oil over the surface.
4. Bake until well-browned and puffy, about 20–25 minutes.

Sausage pizza

MAKES 1

12 oz (350 g) Italian sausages
olive oil
1 quantity deep-dish pizza dough (see page 44)
5 oz (150 g) mozzarella cheese, grated (shredded)
7 oz (200 g) mushrooms, thinly sliced
1 quantity spicy pizza sauce (see page 54)
1 oz (30 g) Parmesan, grated (shredded)

1. Preheat the oven to 450°F/230°C/Gas mark 8.
2. Crumble the sausage meat into a large frying pan over medium-high heat. Cook, stirring often, until lightly browned. Pour off any drippings and discard. Set the sausage aside.
3. Grease a 15 in (37 cm) deep-dish pizza pan and line with dough.
4. Sprinkle half of the mozzarella over the dough. Cover with an even layer of mushrooms, then add the cooked sausage. Spread the sauce over the sausage. Cover with remaining mozzarella and top with the Parmesan.
5. Bake for 20–25 minutes, until browned and bubbling.

Pizza d'Alsace

MAKES 1

2 quantities Neapolitan pizza dough (see page 38)

4 oz (115 g) slab bacon, cubed

1 tablespoon olive oil

1 large onion, thinly sliced

1 egg

1 tablespoon plain (all-purpose)

1 oz (30 g) Gruyère cheese, grated (shredded)

FROMAGE BLANC

6 oz (150 g/¾ cup) ricotta cheese

3 tablespoons plain (natural) yogurt

pinch of salt

1. To prepare the fromage blanc, combine the ricotta, yogurt and salt in a blender and blend for 30 seconds. Chill for 12 hours before using.
2. Preheat the oven to 425°F/220°C/Gas mark 7.
3. Shape the pizza dough into one large round or two smaller ones and transfer to greased baking trays (sheets).
4. In a medium frying pan over moderate heat, cook the bacon in olive oil until well-browned. Transfer the bacon to a plate with a slotted spoon and add the onion to the pan. Sauté until slightly softened (about 5 minutes). Cool to room temperature.
5. Whisk together the fromage blanc, egg and flour.
6. Spread the dough with the topping to within ¾ in (2 cm) of the edge. Top with onions and bacon and scatter with the cheese. Brush the edge of the dough lightly with 2 tablespoons water. Bake until golden brown, 15–20 minutes.

Gorgonzola & prosciutto pizza

MAKES 1

3 cloves garlic, unpeeled
1 quantity basic pizza dough (see page 34)
1 quantity basic tomato sauce (see page 52)
7 oz (200 g) mozzarella cheese, grated (shredded)
1½ oz (45 g) crumbled Gorgonzola cheese, crumbled
4 oz (115 g) sliced prosciutto, cut into strips

1. Preheat the oven to 450°F/230°C/Gas mark 8.
2. Add the garlic to 16 fl oz (475 ml/2 cups) boiling water in a small saucepan, boil for 1 minute. Drain, peel, then thinly slice.
3. Shape the pizza dough and spread the sauce over the dough. Sprinkle with garlic, then with the cheeses. Arrange the prosciutto strips over the top.
4. Bake until the crust is well-browned, 15–20 minutes.

Yogurt chicken pizza

MAKES 1

1 quantity basic pizza dough (see page 34)
½ cup plain (natural) yogurt
¼ cup fresh mint, chopped
1 tablespoon mango chutney
8 oz (225 g) cooked chicken, chopped
1 red capsicum (bell pepper), thinly sliced
¼ cup fresh coriander leaves
3 tablespoons pine nuts

1. Preheat the oven to 400°F/200°C/Gas mark 6.
2. Shape the pizza dough into a 12 in (30 cm) round. Place on a lightly greased baking tray (sheet) and set aside.
3. Put the yogurt, mint and chutney in a bowl and mix to combine. Spread over the pizza base and bake for 15 minutes.
4. Top the pizza with chicken, red capsicum, coriander leaves and pine nuts and bake for 10–15 minutes longer or until the topping is heated through and the base is crisp and golden.

Pizza supremo

MAKES 2

2 quantities basic pizza dough (see page 34)
6 oz (150 g (¾ cup) tomato paste (purée)
1 green capsicum (bell pepper), chopped
5 oz (150 g) pepperoni or salami, sliced
5 oz (150 g) ham or prosciutto, sliced
4 oz (115 g) mushrooms, sliced
14 oz (400 g) can pineapple pieces, drained
2 oz (55 g) pitted olives
4 oz (115 g) mozzarella cheese, grated (shredded)
4 oz (115 g) mature Cheddar cheese, grated (shredded)

1. Preheat the oven to 400°F/200°C/Gas mark 6.
2. Prepare the pizza dough. Divide the dough into two portions and shape each to form a 12 in (30 cm) round. Place each on greased baking trays and spread with tomato paste.
3. Arrange half the green capsicum, pepperoni or salami, ham or prosciutto, mushrooms, pineapple and olives attractively on each pizza base.
4. Combine the cheeses and scatter half the mixture over each pizza. Bake for 25–30 minutes or until the cheese is golden and the base is crisp.

Thai beef pizza

MAKES 2

1 lb (450 g) rump steak, trimmed of all visible fat

2 quantities basic pizza dough (see page 34)

3 tablespoons tomato paste

2 tablespoons sweet chilli sauce

3 spring onions (scallions), chopped

1 carrot, cut into matchsticks

THAI MARINADE

1 clove garlic, crushed

3 tablespoons soy sauce

1 stalk fresh lemongrass, chopped, or 1 teaspoon dried lemongrass, or 1 teaspoon finely grated (shredded) lemon zest

½ cup fresh coriander (cilantro), chopped

1. To make the marinade, place the garlic, soy sauce, lemongrass and coriander in a large bowl and mix to combine. Set aside.
2. Heat a non-stick frying pan over a high heat, add the steak and cook for 1 minute on each side. Remove the steak from the pan, cool and slice thinly. Add the steak to the marinade, cover and set aside for 15 minutes.
3. Preheat the oven to 400°F/200°C/Gas mark 6.
4. Prepare the pizza dough. Shape the dough into two 12 in (30 cm) rounds and place on greased baking trays (sheets).
5. Combine the tomato paste and sweet chilli sauce, spread over the pizza bases and bake for 15 minutes.
6. Top the pizza bases with spring onions and carrot, then arrange the beef slices attractively on top and bake for 10 more minutes, or until topping is heated through and the base is crisp and golden. Garnish with extra spring onion and coriander, to serve.

Pepperoni pizza

MAKES 2

2 quantities basic pizza dough (see page 34)
6 oz (150 g/⅔) cup tomato paste (purée)
7 oz (200 g) button (white) mushrooms, sliced
1 green capsicum (bell pepper), chopped
20 slices pepperoni
20 slices cabanossi sausage
8 oz (225 g) mozzarella cheese, grated (shredded)

1. Preheat the oven to 400°F/200°C/Gas mark 6.
2. Prepare the pizza dough, then shape it into two 12 in (30 cm) rounds and place on greased baking trays (sheets). Spread with tomato paste, then top each base with half the mushrooms and capsicum.
3. Arrange half the pepperoni and cabanossi sausage on each pizza and scatter each half with mozzarella. Bake for 25–30 minutes, or until cheese is golden and base is crisp.

Chicken satay pizza

MAKES 1

14 oz (400 g) chicken thigh fillets, diced
¾ cup satay marinade
1 tablespoon peanut oil
4 spring onions (scallions), sliced
1 carrot, grated (shredded)
3 oz (85 g) snow peas (mangetout), trimmed and sliced
1 large pizza base
2 teaspoons sesame seeds
¼ cup fresh coriander (cilantro) leaves, chopped

1. Preheat the oven to 220°C/425°F/Gas mark 7.
2. Combine the chicken with 4 fl oz (120 ml/½ cup) marinade in a bowl.
3. Heat the oil in a large frying pan over medium to high heat. Cook the chicken for 5 minutes. Stir in the spring onions, carrot and snow peas and cook for 1–2 minutes or until the snow peas turn bright green.
4. Spread the remaining marinade over the pizza base and spoon the chicken over. Sprinkle with sesame seeds. Place on a baking tray (sheet) and bake for 12–15 minutes. Top with the coriander leaves and cut into wedges.

Basil & pork pizza

MAKES 1

12 oz (350 g) lean pork mince
¼ cup fresh basil, chopped
2 cloves garlic, crushed
4 spring onions (scallions), chopped
freshly ground black pepper
3 tablespoons tomato paste (purée)
4 oz (115 g) mozzarella cheese, grated
  (shredded)
1 red capsicum (bell pepper), sliced
12 black olives, pitted

¼ cup fresh parsley, chopped

PIZZA BASE
6½ oz (185 g) cornmeal
4 oz (115 g) self-raising (self-rising) flour
1 teaspoon baking powder
¼ pint (150 ml/⅔ cup) milk

1. Preheat the oven to 350°F/180°C/Gas mark 4.
2. To make the base, place the cornmeal, flour and baking powder in a large
   bowl. Make a well in the centre and gradually pour in the milk, mixing to
   form a sticky dough. Turn the dough onto a lightly floured surface and
   knead for 3–4 minutes. Press into a greased 9 in (23 cm) pizza tray,
   bringing up the edges to form a rim.
3. Place the pork, basil, garlic, spring onions and black pepper, to taste, in a
   bowl and mix to combine. Set aside.
4. Spread the pizza base with tomato paste and top with the meat mixture and
   half the cheese. Arrange the red capsicum and olives attractively on the
   pizza, then sprinkle with the remaining cheese and parsley. Bake for
   45 minutes, or until cooked.

Pizza di Napoli

MAKES 1

1 quantity basic pizza dough (see page 34)
2 fl oz (50 ml/¼ cup) olive oil
2½ fl oz (75 ml/⅓ cup) tomato sauce
1¾ lb (800 g) canned chopped tomatoes
10 oz (300 g) mushrooms, sliced
1 onion, sliced
1 teaspoon salt
1 teaspoon freshly ground black pepper
1 teaspoon dried oregano
12 slices salami
4 oz (115 g) mozzarella cheese, thinly sliced

1. Preheat the oven to 400°F/200°C/Gas mark 6.
2. Prepare the pizza dough, then shape it into a 12 in (30 cm) round and place on a greased baking tray (sheet).
3. For the topping, mix the oil with the tomato sauce and spread over the dough.
4. Cover the pizza base with the tomatoes, mushrooms and onion and season with salt and pepper. Scatte oregano over the vegetables, then arrange slices of salami over the pizza and cover with cheese slices.
5. Bake for 25–30 minutes, or until the cheese is golden and the base is crisp.

Spinach, ham & bacon pizza

MAKES 1

1 quantity basic pizza dough (see page 34)
1 onion, finely chopped
3 oz (85 g) bacon, chopped
3 oz (85 g) ham, diced
2 tablespoons olive oil
1 lb (450 g) fresh spinach, washed and torn

¼ teaspoon ground nutmeg
2 teaspoons lemon juice
14 oz (400 g) tomatoes, sliced
salt and freshly ground black pepper
1 teaspoon dried marjoram
3½ oz (100 g) Gouda cheese

1. Preheat the oven to 400°F/200°C/Gas mark 6.
2. Prepare the pizza dough, then shape it into a 12 in (30 cm) round and place on a greased baking tray (sheet).
3. Heat the oil in a frying pan and cook the onion, bacon and ham for 5 minutes, stirring occasionally.
4. Add the spinach to the pan with the nutmeg and lemon juice and cook for about 3 minutes until the spinach is limp. Squeeze out any extra fluid from the spinach and spread the mixture over the pizza base.
5. Top with sliced tomatoes and season with salt, pepper and marjoram. Sprinkle the cheese over the pizza.
6. Bake for 25–30 minutes, or until the cheese is golden and the base is crisp.

Supreme pizza mozzarella

MAKES 1

1 large red capsicum (bell pepper)
1 eggplant (aubergine), cut in half
1 lb (450 g/2 cups) self-raising (self-rising)
    flour
1 clove garlic, crushed
1 teaspoon dried basil or oregano
4 fl oz (120 ml/½ cup) milk
1 tablespoon olive oil

2 tablespoons tomato paste
4 oz (115 g) salami, cut into strips
1 large tomato, sliced or cut into wedges
14 oz (400 g) can artichoke hearts, drained
    and cut into quarters
10 oz (300 g) mozzarella cheese, grated
    (shredded)
basil leaves

1. Preheat the oven to 400°F/200°C/Gas mark 6.
2. Place the capsicum in a shallow ovenproof dish with the eggplant and 4 fl oz (120 ml/½ cup) of water. Cover and bake for 20 minutes or until soft. Do not turn the oven off. Remove the covering from the vegetables and set aside to cool.
3. Meanwhile, sift the flour into a bowl and add the garlic, oregano, milk and oil. Mix to a soft dough. Place the dough on a floured surface and knead until smooth. Roll out into a circle large enough to cover an greased 11 in (28 cm) pizza tray.
4. Remove the seeds and skin from the capsicum and cut into thick slices. Scoop out the eggplant pulp using a spoon, and place in a bowl. Combine with the tomato paste and spread over the pizza base. Arrange the remaining ingredients on top, finishing with the cheese.
5. Bake in the oven for 20–25 minutes, or until the crust is golden brown and the cheese has melted. Garnish with fresh basil.

Herbed ham pizza

MAKES 1

3 teaspoons sugar

1½ teaspoons active dry yeast

8 oz (225 g/2 cups) wholemeal (whole-wheat) flour

6 oz (150 g/1¼ cups) plain (all-purpose) flour

2 fl oz (50 ml/¼ cup) vegetable oil

2 tablespoons tomato paste

8 fl oz (250 ml/1 cup) basic tomato sauce (see page 52)

4 oz (115 g) lean ham, chopped

1 red capsicum (bell pepper), sliced

4 spring onions (scallions), chopped

2 oz (55 g) mozzarella cheese, grated (shredded)

½ cup fresh parsley, chopped

1. To make the dough, place the sugar, yeast and 2 fl oz (50 ml/¼ cup) water in a bowl and whisk with a fork until the yeast dissolves. Set aside in a warm place for 5 minutes or until the mixture is foamy.
2. Sift the flours together into a bowl. Stir in the oil, yeast mixture and 6 fl oz (175 ml/¾ cup) warm water and mix to make a soft dough. Turn out onto a lightly floured surface and knead for 10 minutes, or until the dough is smooth and glossy.
3. Place the dough in a lightly oiled bowl, cover with cling wrap (cling film) and set aside in a warm draught-free place for 1 hour or until doubled in volume. Punch down the dough and divide into two equal portions.
4. Preheat the oven to 425°F/220°C/Gas mark 7.
5. On a lightly floured surface roll out the dough to form two 12 in (30 cm) rounds. Place the pizza bases on greased baking trays (sheets) and spread with tomato paste. Spread with the pasta sauce and top with the ham and red capsicum. Sprinkle with the spring onions, cheese and parsley and bake for 20 minutes, or until the bases are crisp and cooked.

Ham & mozzarella pizza

MAKES 1

1 quantity basic pizza dough (see page 34)
2 tablespoons olive oil
1 onion, finely chopped
4 large tomatoes, skinned and finely chopped
   (see page 17)
1 bay leaf
1 small sprig thyme
few drops of Tabasco sauce
1 clove garlic, finely chopped
salt and freshly ground black pepper

TOPPING
2 tomatoes, sliced
½ onion, thinly sliced
2 slices lean cooked ham, diced
7 oz (200 g) mozzarella cheese
salt and freshly ground black pepper
1 teaspoon dried oregano
fresh oregano, chopped

1. Preheat the oven to 425°F/220°C/Gas mark 7. To make the tomato sauce, heat the oil in a frying pan and fry the onion until softened. Add the tomatoes, bay leaf, thyme, Tabasco and garlic. Season with salt and pepper and cook for about 30 minutes, stirring frequently.
2. When the liquid from the tomatoes has almost evaporated, remove and discard the bay leaf and the sprig of thyme. Allow the sauce to cool a little, then blend in a food processor until smooth.
3. Roll out the dough into a round, place on a baking tray (sheet) and spread with the prepared tomato sauce.
4. Arrange the sliced tomatoes over the tomato sauce, then top with the onion and ham. Cut the cheese into thin slices and scatter over the pizza. Season with salt and pepper and sprinkle over the oregano.
5. Bake for 15 minutes. Serve immediately garnished with fresh oregano.

Bacon & goat cheese pizza

MAKES 1

1 quantity basic pizza dough (see page 34)
1 quantity basic tomato sauce (page 52)
1 onion, thinly sliced
4 rashers (strips) bacon
2 oz (50 g) goat's cheese
salt and freshly ground black pepper
6 sprigs fresh marjoram, leaves removed and stalks discarded
black olives

1. Preheat the oven to 425°F/220°C/Gas mark 7. Roll out the dough on a lightly floured work surface. Place on a greased baking tray (sheet).
2. Spread the tomato sauce over the dough, then sprinkle over the onion.
3. Cut the bacon into small pieces and scatter over the pizza.
4. Thinly slice the goat's cheese and place the slices over the bacon.
5. Season with salt and pepper, sprinkle over the marjoram and bake for about 15 minutes. Serve hot, garnished with olives.

Individual egg & bacon pizzas

MAKES 4

1 quantity basic pizza dough (see page 34)
1 quantity basic tomato sauce (see page 52)
1 large onion, finely sliced
4 rashers (strips) bacon, cut into small pieces
salt and freshly ground black pepper
4 eggs
1 oz (30 g) Parmesan, grated (shredded)

1. Preheat the oven to 425°F/220°C/Gas mark 7.
2. Divide the dough into four equal pieces. Roll out each on a lightly floured work surface into a thin round. Place each on a baking tray (sheet).
3. Spread about 5 tablespoons of the tomato sauce over each pizza base.
4. Scatter the onion over the tomato sauce, then the bacon. Season with salt and pepper.
5. Break one egg onto the centre of each pizza. Scatter the cheese evenly over each pizza.
6. Bake for about 10–15 minutes. Serve immediately.

Gourmet

Pizzas are great for impromptu entertaining and for feeding a crowd. This collection of recipes made using more exotic ingredients shows just how good these foods are for entertaining. All that is needed to complete a full meal is a fresh salad of mixed lettuces, baby tomatoes and sliced capsicums, all covered with your favourite dressing.

Pizza al pesto e fontina

MAKES 1

3 tablespoons olive oil
8 oz (225 g) mushrooms, thinly sliced
1 quantity basic pizza dough (see page 34)
5 oz (150 g) fontina cheese, grated (shredded)
1 quantity pesto pizza sauce (see page 56)

1. Preheat the oven to 450°F/230°C/Gas mark 8.
2. Heat 2 tablespoons of the oil in large frying pan over medium-high heat. Add the mushrooms and cook, stirring often, until mushrooms are lightly browned and the liquid has evaporated. Remove the pan from the heat.
3. Shape the pizza dough and brush evenly with some of the oil in which the mushrooms were cooked.
4. Scatter the cheese evenly over the dough. Arrange the mushrooms on top and drizzle with the remaining oil.
5. Bake until the crust is well browned, about 25 minutes. Spoon pesto evenly over the pizza. Return to the oven just long enough to heat the pesto (1–2 minutes). Serve hot.

Pizza alla pancetta

MAKES 1

1 tablespoon olive oil
1 red onion, thinly slivered
4 oz (115 g) pancetta, cut into ½ in (12 mm) strips
1 quantity pizza dough (see page 34)
1 quantity basic tomato pizza sauce (see page 52)
5 oz (150 g) mozzarella cheese, grated (shredded)
1 oz (30 g) Romano or Parmesan cheese, grated (shredded)

1. Preheat oven to 450°F/230°C/Gas mark 8.
2. Heat oil in a large frying pan over moderate heat. Add onion and cook, stirring often, until soft but not browned (8–10 minutes). Remove onion with a slotted spoon and reserve.
3. Add pancetta to same pan and cook, stirring often, until it begins to brown (about 3 minutes). Drain on absorbent paper, reserving oil in pan.
4. Brush dough evenly with oil remaining in frying pan. Spread sauce over the pizza. Sprinkle evenly with cheeses. Arrange onion and pancetta evenly over surface.
5. Bake on lowest rack of oven until crust is well-browned (15–20 minutes). Serve hot.

Stuffed pizza

MAKES 1

2 fl oz (50 ml) ¼ cup olive oil
1 onion, thinly sliced
8 oz (225 g) mushrooms, thinly sliced
1 red or green capsicum (bell pepper), sliced
2 cloves garlic, chopped
½ teaspoon salt
½ teaspoon dried oregano
pinch black pepper
pinch dried marjoram

1 quantity deep-dish pizza dough (see page 44)
5 oz (150 g) mild Cheddar cheese, grated (shredded)
1 quantity basic tomato pizza sauce (see page 52)
2 oz (55 g) Parmesan, grated (shredded)

1. Preheat oven to 425°F/220°C/Gas mark 7.
2. In a large frying pan over medium-high heat, heat the olive oil. Add the onion, mushrooms and capsicum and cook, stirring often, until the onion is soft. Stir in the garlic, salt, oregano, pepper and marjoram, then remove from the heat and set aside.
3. Grease a 15 in (37 cm) deep-dish pizza pan. Divide the dough into two portions, one about a third larger than the other. Roll out the larger portion to a 16 in (40 cm) round. Place the dough in the pan, pressing it up the sides.
4. Scatter half the Cheddar cheese over the dough. Spread the vegetable mixture over the cheese.
5. Roll out the remaining dough to a 15 in (37 cm) round and place over the vegetables, folding the rim of dough lining the edges of the pan over the top layer of dough. Spread tomato sauce on top. Sprinkle evenly with the remaining Cheddar. Top with Parmesan.
6. Bake until the crust and cheese are well-browned, 25–30 minutes. Let stand for 2–3 minutes before serving.

Pizza Côte d'Azur

MAKES 1

2 fl oz (50 ml/¼ cup) olive oil
2 onions, thinly sliced
2 cloves garlic, chopped (see page 24)
½ teaspoon dried herbes de Provence
2 fl oz (50 ml/¼cup) flat-leaf parsley, coarsely chopped
1 quantity basic pizza dough (see page 34)
1 quantity basic tomato pizza sauce (see page 52)
4 oz (115 g) Gruyère cheese, grated (shredded)
2 oz (55 g) anchovy fillets, well drained
2 oz (55 gl/¼cup) small niçoise olives

1. Preheat the oven to 450°F/230°C/Gas mark 8.
2. Heat the oil in a large frying pan over moderate heat. Add the onions and cook, stirring often, until soft but not browned, 10–12 minutes, then remove from the heat.
3. Spoon about 1 tablespoon of the hot oil from the pan into a small bowl, then mix in the garlic, herbes de Provence and parsley.
4. Shape the pizza dough, roll out and place on a baking tray (sheet). Scatter evenly with cheese. Spread the onions on top. Arrange the anchovies and olives over the onions. Drizzle over the garlic-and-herb mixture.
5. Bake until crust is well-browned, 20–25 minutes. Serve hot.

NOTE: This pizza is flavoured with herbes de Provence, a commercial blend of dried thyme, lavender, summer savoury, basil and rosemary – herbs typical of the south of France.

Pizza Siciliano

MAKES 1

1 quantity basic pizza dough (see pages 34)
1 quantity garlic-oregano pizza sauce (see page 58)
olive oil
2 red capsicums (bell peppers), roasted and sliced (see page 24)
grated (shredded) Parmesan

1. Preheat the oven to 450°F/230°C/Gas mark 8.
2. Shape the pizza dough on a baking tray (sheet) and spread the sauce on top. Drizzle with olive oil and top with red capsicums.
3. Bake until well-browned and puffy, about 20 minutes. Dust with Parmesan. Serve hot.

Three-cheese pizza

MAKES 1

1 quantity basic pizza dough (see page 34)
2 teaspoons vegetable oil
3½ oz (100 g) blue cheese, crumbled
4 oz (115 g) pine nuts
1¾ oz (50 g) mozzarella cheese, grated (shredded)
1 tablespoon fresh oregano leaves or ½ teaspoon dried oregano
1 oz (30 g) Parmesan, grated (shredded)
freshly ground black pepper

1. Preheat the oven to 400°F/200°C/Gas mark 6.
2. Set aside one quarter of the dough. Roll out the remaining dough to fit a greased 10 x 13 in (25 x 32 cm) baking tray (sheet) and brush with oil.
3. Roll the reserved dough into two sausage shapes each 10 in (25 cm) long. Place these across the pizza base to divide it into three equal portions.
4. Top one third of the pizza with the blue cheese and pine nuts, another third with the mozzarella cheese and oregano and the remaining third with the Parmesan and black pepper, to taste.
5. Bake for 20–25 minutes or until the cheese is golden and the base is crisp. Garnish with fresh basil.

Moroccan lamb pizza

MAKES 4

1 tablespoon sunflower oil
1 re donion, finely chopped
2 cloves garlic, crushed
8 oz (225 g) lean lamb mince
4 fl oz (120 ml/½ cup) canned crushed
  tomatoes
1 teaspoon ground cumin
1 teaspoon ground coriander
1 teaspoon ground cinnamon
¼ cup fresh coriander (cilantro), chopped
1 tablespoon lemon juice
4 pizza bases

2 tablespoons pine nuts, toasted
4 oz (115 g) mozzarella, grated (shredded)
1 cup fresh mint leaves
1 cup fresh flat leaf parsley
freshly ground black pepper
2 tablespoons mango chutney

RAITA
8 fl oz (250 ml/1 cup) natural (palin) yogurt
1 cucumber, grated (shredded)
¼ cup fresh mint, chopped

1. Heat the oil in a frying pan, add the onion and 1 clove of crushed garlic and
   cook over a medium heat for 1 minute. Add the lamb and cook until the
   lamb is browned, breaking the meat up with a fork. Drain any exces oil from
   the pan. Add the tomatoes, cumin, coriander and 2 teapsoons of the lemon
   juice.
2. Preheat the oven to 400°F/200°C/Gas mark 6. Arrange the pizza bases on
   lightly greased baking trays (sheets).
3. Spread the lamb topping over the pizza bases and scatter with pine nuts and
   mozzarella. Bake for 10 minutes or until the cheese has melted and the
   pizzas are heated through.
4. To make the raita, mix the yogurt, grated cucumber, remaining crushed clove
   of garlic and chopped mint in a bowl.
5. Toss the mint and parsley leaves in the remaining lemon juice and season
   with pepper. Serve the pizzas topped with the herb leaves, raita and chutney.

Pissaladière

MAKES 4

3 tablespoons olive oil
1½ oz (45 g) unsalted butter
4 onions, thinly sliced
3 cloves garlic, chopped
1 teaspoon fresh thyme, chopped
salt and freshly ground black pepper

2 oz (55 g) anchovy fillets in oil
15 pitted Kalamata olives
1 quantity basic pizza dough (see page 34)
¼ cup flat leaf parsley, chopped
¼ cup fresh basil, chopped

1. Preheat the oven to 400°F/200°C/Gas mark 6.
2. In a large, heavy-based frying pan set over medium heat, heat 3 tablespoons olive oil and the butter. Add the onions and cook gently for 5 minutes. Add the garlic, thyme, salt and pepper. Cook for 20 minutes, or until the onions are very soft but not brown. Taste and adjust the seasoning, if necessary.
3. Put two anchovy fillets and half the olives in a blender. Add a few drops of olive oil and blend. Add more oil as necessary to make a smooth paste.
4. To assemble the pissaladière, roll out the dough into a square or circle. Transfer to a baking sheet dusted with cornmeal. Spread with anchovy and olive paste and cover with onion slices.
5. Arrange the remaining anchovies over the onions. Arrange the remaining olives on top. Drizzle with a little olive oil and dust with 2 tablespoons each of parsley and basil. Bake until well browned, about 30–35 minutes. Cool slightly, then scatter over the remaining herbs just before serving.

Seafood

Sweet and flavourful, seafood of all kinds adds depth, colour and texture to a pizza topping. You can make fabulous versions at home with fresh, chopped tomatoes and freshly obtained seafood. Some cooked fish should be applied to the pizza just as it comes out of the oven.

Pizza alla vongole

MAKES 1

8 oz (225 g) peeled, deseeded and chopped tomatoes (see page 24)
4 tablespoons olive oil
4 sprigs fresh oregano, leaves removed and finely chopped
1 quantity Neapolitan pizza dough (see page 38)
1 tablespoon chopped garlic (see page 24)
4 fl oz (120 ml/½ cup) dry white wine
1½ lb/750 g small clams or mussels
¼ cup flat-leaf parsley, coarsely chopped

1. Preheat the oven to 475°F/240°C/Gas mark 9.
2. In a small bowl, combine the tomatoes, 2 tablespoons of the olive oil and the oregano, leave to stand for 15 minutes.
3. Shape the pizza dough and place on a greased baking tray (sheet). Brush the dough with 2 tablespoons of the liquid from the tomatoes. Spoon the tomatoes over the dough. Bake until well-browned and puffy, about 18 minutes. Remove from the oven and set aside.
4. Meanwhile, heat the remaining oil over moderately low heat in a frying pan large enough to hold all the clams. Add the garlic and sauté until fragrant but not browned, about 2 minutes. Add the wine, raise the heat to high and bring to the boil.
5. Add the clams, cover and steam until they open, about 3–5 minutes, shaking occasionally. Discard any clams that haven't opened after 5 minutes.
6. Remove the clam meat from the shells and discard the shells. Return the clams to the frying pan. Add the parsley and remove from the heat. Scatter the clams over the baked pizza and serve hot.

Pizza di mare

MAKES 1

4 oz (115 g) shelled and deveined prawns, cut in half lengthwise
4 oz (115 g) scallops, cut in quarters
1½ tablespoons olive oil
2 teaspoons lemon juice
1 teaspoon finely chopped peeled garlic (see page 24)
salt and freshly ground black pepper
½ red onion, thinly sliced
½ zucchini (courgette), thinly sliced
1 quantity basic pizza dough (see page 34)
3 oz (85 g) Gruyère or provolone cheese, grated (shredded)
2½ fl oz (75 ml/⅓ cup) peeled, deseeded and chopped tomatoes
1 oz (30 g) Parmesan, grated (shredded)
¼ cup flat leaf parsley, chopped
1 quantity rouille sauce (see page 60)

1. Preheat the oven to 425°F/220°C/Gas mark 7.
2. In a small bowl toss the prawns, scallops, 1 tablespoon of the olive oil, the lemon juice, ½ teaspoon of the garlic and a twist of salt and pepper. Marinate for 30–45 minutes. Drain and discard the marinade. Set the shellfish mixture aside.
3. Heat the remaining olive oil in a frying pan. Add the rest of the garlic and onion. Cook for about 20 seconds over high heat, stirring constantly. Add the zucchini and cook, stirring constantly for another 10 seconds. Remove from the heat and set aside.
4. Shape the pizza dough, place on a greased baking tray (sheet) and brush with olive oil. Sprinkle 1the Gruyère cheese over the top. Sprinkle with salt and pepper.
5. Bake until the crust is well-browned,15–20 minutes. Remove the pizza from the oven and preheat the grill (broiler). Scatter the tomatoes, zucchini, onion and seafood over the pizza. Place under the grill until the seafood is almost done (1–2 minutes).
6. Remove the pizza from oven and spoon Rouille Sauce over the top. Sprinkle with Parmesan and pepper. Return the pizza to the grill until the sauce is bubbly, about 2 minutes. Remove and scatter with parsley. Let rest 5 minutes before serving.

Salmon & avocado pizza

MAKES 1

1 quantity basic pizza dough (see page 34)
7 oz (200 g) ricotta cheese, drained
2 tablespoons fresh dill, chopped
1 tablespoon fresh lemon thyme, chopped
8 oz (225 g) smoked salmon, sliced
1 avocado, sliced
1 tablespoon capers, drained
4 oz (115 g) cherry tomatoes, halved

1. Preheat the oven to 400°F/200°C/Gas mark 6.
2. Prepare the pizza dough, then press it into a greased 9 x 13 in (26 x 32 cm) Swiss roll tin (jelly roll pan). Set aside.
3. Place the ricotta cheese, dill and thyme in a bowl and mix to combine. Spread the ricotta mixture over the pizza base and bake for 15 minutes.
4. Top the pizza with smoked salmon, avocado slices, capers and tomatoes. Reduce the oven temperature to 350°F/180°C/Gas mark 4 and bake for 10 minutes more,or until heated through and the base is crisp and golden.

Smoked salmon pizza

MAKES 4

1 quantity basic pizza dough (see page 34)
1 tablespoon olive oil
7 oz (200 g) smoked salmon slices
freshly ground black pepper
4 tablespoons crème fraîche or sour cream
4 teaspoons salmon caviar
¼ cup fresh lemon thyme, chopped

1. Preheat the oven to 400°F/200°C/Gas mark 6.
2. Divide the pizza dough into four portions and shape each to form a 6 in (15 cm) round. Place the rounds on lightly greased baking trays (sheets), brush with oil and bake for 15 minutes or until crisp and golden.
3. Reduce the oven temperature to 350°F/180°C/Gas mark 4. Top the pizzas with smoked salmon and black pepper, to taste, and bake for 8 minutes or until the salmon is hot.
4. Top the pizzas with crème fraîche and caviar and sprinkle with thyme.

Anchovy & onion pizza

MAKES 2

1 quantity basic pizza dough (see page 34)
1 quantity basic tomato sauce (see page 52)
2 large onions, thinly sliced
16 anchovy fillets
salt and freshly ground black pepper
fresh herb sprigs

1. Preheat the oven to 425°F/220°C/Gas mark 7. Roll out the dough into 2 rounds. Place on greased baking trays.
2. Spread the tomato sauce evenly over the pizzas.
3. Arrange the sliced onion over the sauce and place the anchovy fillets neatly over the onion.
4. Season with salt and pepper. Bake for about 20 minutes, or until crisp and cooked. Serve immediately, garnished with fresh herb sprigs.

Seafood pizza

MAKES 1

8 oz (225 g) fresh cockles
16 oz (500 g) fresh mussels
4 fl oz (120 ml/½ cup) white wine
1 quantity basic pizza dough (see page 34)
1 quantity basic tomato sauce (see page 52)

1 large onion, thinly sliced
2 cloves garlic, chopped (see page 24)
1 teaspoon dried marjoram
salt and freshly ground black pepper
1 oz (30 g) Parmesan, grated (shredded)

1. Wash, brush and rinse the cockles and mussels thoroughly. Place them in a large saucepan, pour over the wine and place over a high heat, shaking the pan frequently until all the shells have opened. Set the pan aside to allow the contents to cool.
2. Once the cockles and mussels are cooled, remove from their shells, discarding any that have not opened. Discard the juices.
3. Preheat the oven to 425°F/220°C/Gas mark 7. Roll out the pizza dough into a large round on a lightly floured work surface. Place on a baking tray (sheet).
4. Pour the tomato sauce into the centre of the pizza and spread over the dough with the back of a spoon.
5. Place the sliced onion over the tomato sauce, then place the mussels and cockles on top.
6. Scatter over the garlic, season with marjoram and salt and pepper and top with Parmesan.
7. Bake for about 15–25 minutes, depending on the thickness of the dough. Serve immediately.

Sardine, lime & coriander

MAKES 1

1 quantity basic pizza dough (see page 34)
2 teaspoons olive oil
3 red onions, sliced
3 cloves garlic, crushed
½ cup fresh coriander (cilantro), chopped
7 oz (200 g) can sardines, drained
1 tablespoon lime juice
freshly ground black pepper

1. Preheat the oven to 425°F/220°C/Gas mark 7.
2. Roll out the pizza dough, then place it on a greased baking tray (sheet) and set aside.
3. To make the topping, heat the oil in a frying pan over a low heat. Add the onions and garlic and cook, stirring, for 5 minutes or until the onions are soft. Add the coriander and mix to combine.
4. Spread the onion mixture over the pizza base, top with sardines, sprinkle with lime juice and black pepper to taste. Bake for 10 minutes, then reduce the oven temperature to 375°F/190°/Gas mark 5 and bake for 15 minutes longer, or until base is crisp and golden.

Sweet

This fun pizza-shaped collection of desserts is perfect for serving to a crowd. Decadent brownies and sweet doughs are lavished with simple but effective ice cream and sweet sauces turning them into delicious tempting treats and a fitting finale for a meal.

Triple-chocolate brownie pizza

MAKES 1

16 oz (500 g) semi-sweet (plain) chocolate,
    chopped
2 z (55 g) unsweetened cocoa powder
2 oz (55 g) unsalted butter
5 eggs
10½ oz (215 g) caster (superfine) sugar
1½ teaspoons vanilla extract
4 oz (115 g) plain (all-purpose) flour, sifted

½ teaspoon baking powder
pinch of salt
8 oz (225 g) chocolate chips
8 oz (225 g) walnuts, chopped
3 scoops vanilla ice cream
3 scoops chocolate ice cream
hocolate sauce, to taste

1. Preheat the oven to 350°F/180°C/Gas mark 4. Generously coat a 16 in (40 cm) pizza pan with butter or oil.
2. In a saucepan over low heat, melt the chocolate, cocoa and butter, stirring until smooth. Remove from the heat and set aside to cool for 5 minutes.
3. In a large bowl, beat the eggs and sugar with an electric mixer until thick and pale. Stir in the vanilla and cooled chocolate mixture, blend well and set aside.
4. Combine the flour, baking powder and salt. Add to the chocolate mixture, stirring just to combine. Fold in the chocolate chips and nuts. Spread the mixture in the prepared pizza pan. Bake for 30 minutes, then remove from the oven. Serve with scoops of vanilla and chocolate ice cream and chocolate sauce.

Chocolate cherry cookie pizza

MAKES 1

3 oz (85 g) butter, softened
3½ oz (100 g) firmly packed brown sugar
1 teaspoon vanilla extract
4 oz (115 g/1 cup) plain (all-purpose)
6 oz (175 g) semi-sweet (plain) chocolate, coarsely chopped
2 oz (55 g/½ cup) pecans, coarsely chopped
2 oz (55 g/⅓ cup) red candied cherries, halved
icing (confectioners') sugar, to dust

1. Preheat the oven to 375°F/190°C/Gas mark 5. Generously coat a 12 in (30 cm) pizza pan with olive oil.
2. In a large mixing bowl, beat the butter and brown sugar until light and fluffy. Stir in the vanilla, then gradually add the flour, mixing until blended. Stir in the chocolate, pecans and cherries.
3. Tip the mixture into the prepared pizza pan and use your fingers to push it to within ¼ in (6 mm) of the outer edge.
4. Bake until well-browned, 14–16 minutes. Cool for 10 minutes in the pan on a wire rack. Sprinkle lightly with icing sugar. Remove from the pan when cool.

Almond raspberry ice cream pizza

MAKES 1

10 oz (300 g) slivered almonds
6 oz (175 g) unsalted butter, at room
  temperature
2½ oz (65 g) sugar
6 oz (150 g/1½ cups) plain (all-purpose) flour
1 egg, lightly beaten
1 teaspoon almond extract

½ teaspoon vanilla extract
pinch of salt
bottled berry syrup, to taste
3 scoops berry ice cream
4 oz (115 g/1 cup) almonds, toasted and
  chopped

1. Generously grease a 16 in (40 cm) pizza pan
2. Combine the almonds, butter, sugar, flour, egg, almond and vanilla extract
   and salt in a bowl. Mix well.
3. Press the dough evenly into the pan, leaving a ¼ in (6 mm) border around
   the edge to allow the crust to expand while baking. Chill for 30 minutes.
4. Preheat the oven to 380°F/190°C/Gas mark 5.
5. Remove from the refrigerator and bake until golden brown, about
   20 minutes. Leave to set in the pan, then turn out on to a wire rack to
   go cold.
6. With a spatula, spread berry syrup over the cooled crust. Top with small
   scoops of berry ice cream. Sprinkle chopped, toasted nuts over the ice
   cream and serve at once.

Pizza galette

MAKES 1

¼ oz (7 g) active dry yeast
3½ oz (100 g/½ cup) sugar, plus 5 tablespoons to decorate
4 oz (115 g) butter, softened, plus 1 oz (30 g) to decorate
1 teaspoon lemon zest
1 egg
pinch of salt
7 oz (200 g/1¾ cups) plain (all-purpose) flour
olive oil

1. Sprinkle the yeast over the 2 fl oz (50 ml/¼ cup) warm water in a small bowl. Add 1 tablespoon of the sugar. Let stand until the yeast is soft (about 5 minutes).
2. In the bowl of an electric mixer, cream the butter with 2 tablespoons of sugar until fluffy. Blend in the lemon zest, then the egg.
3. Stir the salt into the yeast mixture, then blend into the butter mixture. Gradually blend in the flour to make a soft dough. Continue beating until the dough is smooth and elastic (about 5 minutes).
4. Place the dough in a buttered bowl. Cover with cling wrap (cling film) and leave to rise in a warm place until doubled in bulk (about 1½ hours). Punch dough down. Roll the dough on a well-floured surface into a circle about 12 in (30 cm) in diameter.
5. Preheat the oven to 425°F/220°C/Gas mark 7. Oil a 16 in (40 cm) pizza pan. Pat and stretch the dough to fit the pan, pinching the edge to make a slightly raised rim. Cut the remaining 1 oz (30 g) butter into 24 equal pieces and distribute evenly over the dough. Sprinkle with the remaining 5 tablespoons of sugar.
6. Bake until well browned,12–15 minutes. Cut into wedges and serve warm.

Index

Published in 2014 by
New Holland Publishers
London • Sydney • Cape Town • Auckland

The Chandlery Unit 114 50 Westminster Bridge Road London SE1 7QY
1/66 Gibbes Street Chatswood NSW 2067 Australia
Wembley Square First Floor Solan Road Gardens Cape Town 8001 South Africa
218 Lake Road Northcote Auckland New Zealand

Copyright © 2014 New Holland Publishers

www.newhollandpublishers.com

A catalogue record of this book is available at the British Library and the National
Library of Australia.

ISBN: 9781742574851

Publisher: Fiona Schultz
Design: Lorena Susak
Production Director: Olga Dementiev
Printer: Toppan Leefung Printing Ltd (China)

10 9 8 7 6 5 4 3 2 1

Texture: Shutterstock

Follow New Holland Publishers on
Facebook: www.facebook.com/NewHollandPublishers

UK £9.99
US $14.99